AXIS OF DECEIT

To John,

AndyWilkie

1 August 2004

AXIS OF DECEIT

ANDREW WILKIE

Published by Black Inc. Agenda
Series Editor: Robert Manne

Other books in the Black Inc. Agenda series:

*Whitewash: On Keith Windschuttle's
Fabrication of Aboriginal History*

The Howard Years

An imprint of Schwartz Publishing
Level 5, 289 Flinders Lane
Melbourne Victoria 3000 Australia
email: enquiries@blackincbooks.com
web: http://www.blackincbooks.com

Index by Michael Ramsden

National Library of Australia Cataloguing-in-Publication entry:

Wilkie, Andrew.
Axis of deceit.

Includes index.
ISBN 0 9750769 2 2.

1. Wilkie, Andrew. 2. Australia. Office of National
Assessments. 3. Iraq War, 2003 - Personal narratives,
Australian. 4. Iraq War, 2003 - Causes. 5. Whistle
blowing - Australia. 6. Intelligence officers - Australia -
Biography. 7. Intelligence service - Australia. 8.
Australia - Politics and government - 21st century. I.
Australia. Office of National Assessments. II. Title.

956.70443

CONTENTS

Dedicated to the victims of the Iraq war.
May you rest in peace.

And may those whose lies killed you be one day brought to
justice.

PROLOGUE

There is nothing in man's plight that his vision, if he cared to cultivate it, could not alleviate. The challenge is to see what could be done, and then to have the heart and the resolution to attempt it.
—George Kennan

I was a lieutenant colonel and a senior intelligence officer. My great-uncle was killed at the Mennen Gate in Belgium during World War I – the war they said would end all wars. More of my kin served in the next big one: my father completed 32 missions over German-occupied Europe as a tail-gunner in Lancaster heavy bombers, while my mother served in the Women's Australian Auxiliary Air Force. My brother fought in South Vietnam. More recently my friends have served all over the world. My wife spent almost a year on operational service in Cambodia.

Now I've written a book condemning the war in Iraq and the governments that made it happen. No-one is more surprised about that than I am. I was brought up in a conservative Catholic family in regional Australia. I enlisted in the Australian Army as soon as I finished high school, trained at the Royal Military College Duntroon and enjoyed a successful military career before being medically discharged with injured knees. My post-Army working life was dominated by the world of intelligence. Even my stint in private enterprise, working for US defence giant Raytheon in management and business development, was pretty straight. What the course of my life shows, I think, is that a time can come unexpectedly in any life when certain things – call them principles or fundamental beliefs – become more important than anything else. What is ultimately most precious is the opportunity to help make the world a better place.

The pages of history are already filled with unnecessary wars and criminals dressed up as patriots. The history of the present-day will be no different, no matter what happens in the future, because the war in Iraq that began in March 2003 was neither justified nor legal. Not justified because Iraq did not pose a serious enough security threat to any other country to warrant a war. Not legal because Iraq's material breach of United Nations Security Council Resolution 1441 did not present a legal basis for resort to force.

As the war grinds on into its second year, some are inclined to put all of that behind us – to accept that what was done is done and focus instead on helping the people of Iraq to stabilise and repair their country. It is true that we ought to do whatever we can to repair the terrible mess we've made. But it is just as important that we not forget or walk away from the official deception that brought about this war and has been used to justify it ever since. The dishonesty is too serious, the implications too alarming. We were told that there was an urgent need to invade Iraq because Saddam Hussein possessed horrific weapons and it was inevitable that he would hand them on to terrorists.

That story was always arguable, and is now laughable. What is not laughable is the knowledge that at almost every turn the protagonists of the Iraq misadventure looked us straight in the eye and then lied through their teeth. It is well for them that they are protected by victors' justice, because in other places and at other times leaders like them have faced judgement for less.

I didn't find it difficult to reach the conclusions I did before the war began. The raw intelligence on Iraq was sometimes awful and the subsequent assessments were not always much better. Nor did the so-called 'politicisation' of the intelligence community help – that combination of direct political interference and implied expectations which skews intelligence officers' work to suit their political masters. But the reality of the situation in Iraq was always obvious enough to cut through the intelligence clutter in Washington, London and Canberra. Or at least it was to those genuinely interested in knowing the truth.

Even more obvious to me, and to my colleagues, was the significant gap between what we were seeing, and what George W. Bush, Tony Blair and John Howard were saying publicly. This was no small matter. On the one hand was the limited and manageable threat posed by Iraq, while on the other was all that talk about an urgent need to deal with a ruthless dictator before he used his massive arsenal of the world's most deadly weapons.

The only difficult part for me was working out what to do about the gulf between the reality and the spin. That decision had nothing to do with the world of intelligence, but everything to do with my sense of right and wrong, and my threshold for when well-intentioned half-truths become unacceptable lies.

It was, I suppose, a convergence of everything that had shaped my approach to the world – my home life, schooling, military and intelligence service, my relationships with friends and adversaries, and everything else that has influenced me over the years. This made my concern with the government's conduct over Iraq an intensely personal matter, one that might have been dealt with quite differently by anyone else if he or she had found themselves in my exact position.

The personal implications of my decision to stand up to the government are yet to become clear. I've been vilified. I'm emotionally exhausted. I've lost friends. There is no chance of ever returning to a career I cherished. The financial cost is alarming. But even so I have no regrets about what I did, and I would do it all again. Better for me to have done what I could to energise the public debate about the impending conflict than to slip away quietly or to continue with my duties as though nothing were at stake. I wouldn't have been able to live with myself had I failed to act as I did.

Thank you to everyone who has supported me since I took my stand. Your encouragement has kept me going through some difficult times. Mentioning particular people risks offending many more than it heartens, but I want nevertheless to acknowledge all of the members of my family, in particular my wife, Simone, whom I put in an awkward position during 2003 when she was the first woman Commanding Officer of Duntroon.

Invariably relationships suffer terribly from the pressures, buffeting and personal changes that accompany an act of whistle-blowing. Simone and I are no exception, my resignation and its aftermath taking a toll on our marriage. We lived apart during some of this story, at the time apparently for reasons unrelated to my decision to speak out. On reflection, though, I understand that our separation was linked, to some degree, to my great unease concerning the impending war and my inability to do much about it as long as I was living in the CO's house at Duntroon.

I also wish to recognise those serving and former members of the intelligence and defence communities who share many of my concerns. The unease over the government's behaviour runs deep. From their numbers my friend and former colleague Dr Kate Burton has been especially influential.

On 25 August 2003 the Prime Minister invited me to back up my accusation that the government had lied about the Iraq war. He said that:

> If Mr Wilkie has evidence that the Government misrepresented intelligence he should submit it. It is open to him to do so without breaching his legal obligations not to reveal classified information obtained in the course of his previous employment. To suggest otherwise is absurd.

This was a foolish thing for Howard to say – it should be obvious that I don't possess copies of the highly sensitive material that illustrates the government deceit which I discuss in this book. It was also irresponsible, because national security material should be protected as far as possible, so as not to compromise intelligence capabilities and sources. If I do inadvertently brush up against such information here, it is done only in the context of the Prime Minister's invitation to go much further.

Andrew Wilkie, 2004

TAKING A STAND

In this business, whose side do you take?
—A former colleague, before the war

I can't recall precisely the origin of my decision to betray my government. Probably it was during November and December 2002, when I prepared the detailed intelligence assessment for the Australian government of the possible humanitarian consequences of the looming invasion of Iraq. It was a sobering experience, one that left me with a clear sense of how bad the fall-out from the war could easily be.

2003 brought more wake-up calls. On my return from a short holiday in New Zealand with my wife, I began to think more and more about the case for war being put forward by the governments of the United States, United Kingdom and Australia. Too much of it simply didn't add up; like the polished but misleading address delivered to the Australian Parliament by Prime Minister John Howard on 4 February, and the equally dishonest presentation to the United Nations Security Council by US Secretary of State Colin Powell on 5 February.

Looked at sceptically, much of the earlier material that had been released to the public was equally dubious. The September 2002 dossier, *Iraq's Weapons of Mass Destruction: The Assessment of the British Government*, seemed particularly weak, not least because of the way in which serious gaps had been backfilled with reams of allegations that I knew couldn't possibly be supported by hard intelligence. US President George W. Bush's October 2002 remarks in Cincinnati seemed especially gross exaggerations – for instance, his comment that, 'Facing clear evidence of peril, we cannot wait for the final proof – the smoking gun – that could come in the form of a mushroom cloud.'[1]

By early 2003, as part of my work as the Senior Transnational Issues Analyst at the Office of National Assessments (ONA), I was spending considerable time trawling through the vast intelligence database on Iraq so as to be ready to help cover the war once it started. But now I used my research to question what had been unquestionable for so long. What jumped out at me was that the war had little to do with weapons of mass destruction (WMD), and almost nothing to do with al Qaida. We were on the cusp of waging an unjustified war on the basis of a preposterous lie.

That I had developed a more critical eye than some of my intelligence colleagues is unsurprising. After all, I was in a privileged position – as an ex-Australian Army officer I understood war fighting and how fine the line is between victory and defeat; while as an intelligence officer I'd worked on an unusually broad range of issues, including WMD, terrorism and humanitarian matters. Importantly, my work with ONA on transnational issues, such as people-smuggling, had exposed me to some raw intelligence of very poor quality, which gave me a more critical eye in general when it came to analysing intelligence information –

the information we received on the smugglers was frequently uncorroborated and wildly inaccurate, just like much of the material the Americans were collecting on Iraq.

It was not as if no-one else cared. Polling in many countries showed strong opposition to the looming war. In mid-February millions of people around the world took to the streets in an unprecedented show of public concern. Sensible people everywhere suspected that they were being deceived. Even in the intelligence and defence communities there were obvious and widespread misgivings, especially at the analyst level, where talk about the veracity or otherwise of the case for war was not uncommon in cafés or around dinner-tables.

During this time I made what was to be my last trip overseas for the Office of National Assessments, departing on 11 February 2003 for Indonesia, Vietnam, Sri Lanka and Papua New Guinea. The time away did me good, not least because it gave me the long periods of solitude I needed to analyse properly the case for war – in fact I still have some of the notes I scrawled on letterhead paper from Singapore Airlines and the Lanka Oberoi Hotel detailing my accumulating concerns and possible courses of action. During this period I had spirited discussions about Iraq with many people – officials, diplomats and spies. Of course, if they had known or suspected the reason for my preoccupation, they would have viewed our conversations in a quite different light.

Yet to decide what to do, I returned to Australia on 27 February, knowing full well that I would need to move quickly if I was to have any hope of making a difference to the policy and public debate. By this time, although the US and the UK were continuing to bully and bribe the other members of the UN Security Council, it was widely known within the intelligence community that war was inevitable and would commence any time from mid-March. I set Friday, 7 March 2003 as my deadline for going to the media.

For the next week I dreaded the arrival of that day. What helped confirm me in my decision were the insights I gained as I continued to work through the database on Iraq. Every day I became more confident in my assessment that a war could in no way be justified. No matter which way I looked at the issue, both the raw intelligence and the assessments of this intelligence indicated clearly that Iraq did not pose a serious enough security threat to justify a war. Iraq's conventional military was weak, its WMD programme was disjointed and contained, and there was no active co-operation between it and al Qaida.

When 7 March arrived, though, I had the feeling of being in a bad movie. The moment of action had arrived, but I was still unsure how I should proceed. Adding to the anguish was my sense that I was starting to behave suspiciously – not a good look for an intelligence officer sitting at a desk literally covered with some of the most sensitive national security material in the country.

Final resolution by mid-morning was surprisingly easy. In the end, all that was needed was to push aside my detailed concerns and analysis and to ask myself, 'What's your heart telling you to do?' At once I knew the answer. I had to act if I was to be able to live with myself. It was as simple as that. In the end, the big decision was reduced to a gut feeling about right and wrong.

I grabbed a 'with compliments' slip and wrote on it, 'I'd appreciate your giving me a call on 0417 ... out of work hours.' Next I stapled my business card to it, pushed it into my Filofax diary alongside the notes I'd made overseas on Iraq, and headed for the door. ONA employees are subject to random searches;

the difficulty I'd have explaining the contents of my diary was not lost on me. But there was no search that time and I was gone.

I'd realised many days earlier, while in Colombo I think, that if I was to resign I had to make it count. I'd need to get in touch with a high-profile journalist, one who could guarantee me top billing in both print and television. And it had to be someone I could contact directly. If I'd learnt one thing in the intelligence world, it was the importance of letting as few people as possible in on a secret – just one person in the loop without a genuine need to know sends the risk of being compromised soaring. My play was going to be difficult enough without building in extra risks.

The political journalist Laurie Oakes seemed to fit the bill. I liked his work and knew roughly where he lived. His home in the leafy Canberra suburb of Deakin was close to my own, and we'd crossed paths from time to time while walking our dogs in the nearby Red Hill nature reserve. Little did Oakes know that the stranger with the two beagles whom he might have noticed occasionally would end up as another one of his scoops.

First stop after leaving ONA on 7 March was the Deakin newsagent to buy a plain envelope for my note and business card. Next, a nearby phone booth to check on Oakes' address and make a confirmatory call to his number. Instantly I recognised the distinctive voice on his answering machine. So far so good.

Pulling up in Oakes' driveway, all I could think about was whether I was under suspicion already or whether Oakes himself was under surveillance for some reason. After all, he'd been in the thick of some big issues over the years. To be on the safe side I pulled well into his circular driveway behind the bushes and thrust my envelope into his letterbox, pausing only long enough to see if anyone was watching the house or me. An old car was parked across the road but nothing about it looked suspicious, not that I'd really know. In seconds my work was done and I was off. There was definitely no turning back now.

Of course I had no idea when Oakes would call, if ever. But I assumed it was just a matter of time. After all, he hadn't become the big man of Australian journalism by lacking the ability to recognise the significance of a covert approach from someone in the country's senior intelligence agency in the build-up to a controversial war. But what if he was away from Canberra, maybe overseas?

I didn't have to wait long. Oakes rang me at about 9.00 that night, very soon after he'd got home and found my note. At the time I was hosting five of my ONA colleagues to Indian take-away, including the lead Iraq analyst. Suffice to say I took the call elsewhere in the house; not that it amounted to much more than Oakes saying he'd got my note, and me saying I couldn't tell him over the phone what it was about except that I needed to meet with him over the weekend. He offered to meet me any place, any time, and we agreed that he would come to my apartment on Saturday morning.

Deceiving my friends that night wasn't easy. Nor was it any better the following evening when I had dinner with some long-time friends, the executive assistant to John Howard's Chief of Staff and her partner. Later the partner recalled that I seemed uncharacteristically subdued that night – and no wonder. I was uneasy about my duplicity but saw no other option. In the background was something much bigger than my friends and myself: the pre-emptive invasion of a sovereign state, without UN endorsement, for fraudulent reasons. I hope that one day those I seriously offended can come to understand my position, and my decision.

Working through the issue with Oakes was unexpectedly easy. On Saturday, 8 March we met for only an hour or so, covering little more than introductions and, in fairly general terms, my concerns. On Sunday morning we went into more detail, although again the meeting was brief – no more than a couple of hours. At the beginning of that second session Oakes went to some trouble to satisfy himself that I was absolutely committed to resigning from ONA and going to the media. Remarkably, he offered to walk away from the story if I wanted to bail out – a decent chap, the more so for the fact that by then he'd spoken to Garry Linnell, the editor-in-chief of Australia's premier weekly current affairs magazine, the *Bulletin*. Linnell was keen to run the article, probably as the week's cover story.

Both sessions with Oakes, along with the filming of a television interview to be screened on the day I resigned, were conducted in the privacy of my apartment in Kingston, where there was little chance of getting caught out. Much more of a problem was the need for a photograph to accompany the *Bulletin* article. For that the magazine despatched a freelance photographer from Sydney to take a number of shots of me wearing a suit in landmark locations, including in front of Parliament House and by Lake Burley Griffin. I spent the whole of that Sunday afternoon session sweating on the possibility of someone who knew me wandering past and asking what on earth I was up to. That this didn't eventuate was a blessing, not least because I don't recall that I ever came up with a satisfactory response. Fortunately the gathering storm clouds that gave the chosen photograph a sombre effect also cut the session short.

On Monday and Tuesday, my last two days as an intelligence officer, I was surprisingly calm. I'd made my decision and the consequences were unfolding around me; I couldn't have done anything to reverse the course of events by then even if I had changed my mind. On Monday night the *Bulletin* began rolling off the presses, though not before its lawyers had scoured the article and adjusted it to keep everyone out of jail – getting it wrong could have put Linnell, Oakes and me in prison for years under the *Crimes Act*. Some consolation at least was that the journalist, editor and publisher would all have been liable for seven years' jail if they'd disclosed national security material; while I'd have only gone in for two years if found guilty of supplying the information to them in the first place. Make of that what you will.

Secrecy was vitally important during those last couple of days, not least because the government could have tried to stop publication of the *Bulletin* if they'd got wind of its contents. Distribution of the magazine was delayed until as late as possible, and I held off announcing my resignation until 5.00 p.m. on my final day at ONA – just before the pre-recorded news interview was scheduled to go to air and well into the distribution process of the magazine. This provided ammunition later for critics who singled out my contact with the media prior to my actual resignation and accused me of a calculating approach. I think these people miss the point: the issue at the heart of the matter – justification for going to war – was more important than what they thought was appropriate behaviour on my part.

Much about those last days was remarkably routine. I took part in a meeting of the Transnational Issues Branch just before lunch on Monday morning, followed by a meeting with the newly established Australian Crime Commission in the afternoon. Much less routine was the need to prepare my office for my last departure – in-trays to be cleared, safe sorted and outstanding emails actioned. Key documents such as my work passports were left in an obvious spot in my safe for my colleagues to find easily later.

Similar care needed to be taken at home – I had no idea what would happen to me once I showed my hand, and detention for a time was not out of the question. I was, after all, working for a government prepared to lock up asylum seekers indefinitely. So bills were paid and everything tidied up. I even gave a key to my apartment to an ONA friend in case I went to jail and needed someone to help me out.

My final ONA appointment was a planning conference on Iraq at 4.30 p.m. on Tuesday 11 March, which was attended by a dozen or so ONA officers including Kim Jones, the Director-General. The meeting had been called to finalise arrangements for the operation of the National Intelligence Watch Office, a specialised facility within ONA that adjoins its elaborate communications centre. The Watch Office is activated from time to time to provide constant coverage of the most important overseas events. Last opened in the aftermath of the Bali bombing, the National Intelligence Watch Office was now being readied for a war judged most likely to last only a week or so, but which many in ONA suspected could go on for much longer.

Not long after the meeting began, a siren went off throughout the building, followed by an announcement that members of the media were out front and no-one was to leave until further notice. A groan went up. It was too close to knock-off time for the precaution, which was designed to safeguard the identity of ASIO officers (with whom ONA shares its building), to be a popular one. And it wasn't just those inside who would be inconvenienced – the special lights outside the building would also have come on to warn off any colleagues who were intending to re-enter the facility. By now I was feeling pretty uncomfortable, as I knew I'd caused the building shutdown. Oakes had told me earlier that he would set up outside the building in the hope of catching me being hauled out, possibly in custody.

At about 5.00 p.m. Jones left the meeting to return to his office. I waited a moment and then left too. First I went to my office to send a pre-prepared email to my ONA friends, log off and lock my safe. Instantly half a dozen or so of my colleagues had my message waiting on their desktops: 'By the time you read this I'll be gone and you'll understand why. I apologise for any angst this will cause you. Regards, Andrew.'

As I walked up the corridor to Jones' office, I was trembling. Words can't describe how much I respected Jones or how upset I was at this moment. I was about to let him down in an unimaginable way.

'Excuse me Kim, I need to speak with you straightaway about a very important matter ... Do you mind if I close the door? ... I suggest you sit down ... There's no easy way to tell you this, but I've gone to the media to voice my opposition to a war in Iraq. It'll be on tonight's Channel Nine news and in tomorrow's *Bulletin*. Here's my resignation ...'

'I can't believe you've done this ... Do you know the damage this will do? ...'

Little more was said. I was in no shape to talk, and Jones obviously needed to advise Howard's office. It was probably the worst moment of my life. With tears welling up in my eyes, I excused myself and walked out, only to be stopped briefly by Jones – a good man right to the end – and thanked for giving him some warning. He is another person who I hope will one day understand my decision.

Getting out of the building was as easy as walking out the door. Or at least it would have been if the media weren't still out front and the building wasn't still sealed. That was something I needed to fix fast, so I rang Oakes from my office and asked him to pack up. Besides, I was in no state to do an interview. All I really felt like doing was bawling my eyes out. He understood and agreed to leave, though when I went downstairs to the foyer I still had to wait for five minutes among the many restless ASIO and ONA officers, some of whom had now been waiting for three-quarters of an hour. When finally we could leave, I simply slid my bundle of security passes to the mystified ASIO guard through the gap at the base of his bulletproof-glass window and was gone.

I arrived home a little later believing that most of my work for the day was done. I knew I needed to call some members of my family and some friends to tell them what I'd done. Then perhaps there would be time to take stock and gather my strength. I assumed I'd get some requests for interviews that I could put off until the following day. How naive I was. When the Channel Nine national news screened interstate at 6.00 p.m., my phone went into instant overload and stayed that way for many days. I tried for a short time to answer the calls but soon realised that multiple voicemails were being logged for every call I took – I wasn't even keeping up. Amid the confusion I stumbled on the practice of screening most calls through my voicemail and keeping a log. That way I could at least give priority to the most important among the onslaught of calls.

Events took an unforeseen turn at about 7.10 p.m., when Kerry O'Brien, anchor of Australia's flagship current affairs show *The 7.30 Report*, rang to urge me to appear on his programme, by then only some 20 minutes away from broadcast. It was a ridiculous proposal because I was a wreck and had yet to work up any kind of strategy for dealing with the media. For reasons

I still don't understand, I said yes, although I knew even at the time that walking in cold to face O'Brien on live national television was close to the riskiest thing I could do.

At least there was no time to fret. In fact I'd only just enough time to tidy up, scribble in my diary some memory joggers and meet the car the ABC despatched for the short trip to their Parliament House facility. On arrival a short pause at the security checkpoint then straight to my seat in the studio where an earpiece was positioned and thick make-up applied. Seemingly at once the programme's distinctive theme music was coming through the earphone. It was starting. No sign of O'Brien – he was in another studio, Sydney I suppose, leaving me in front of a camera and lights feeling like a kangaroo stuck in a shooter's spotlight. Someone pushed into my hand a copy of the ONA press release concerning my resignation. I knew nothing about Iraq – that was the gist of it. There was no time to think, only react. Every skill I possessed was being tested to the limit. My years of Army service were a strength, although for not the last time I wished I could curl up tightly into a ball.

'Welcome to the programme. Many Australians have been voicing their concern about this country's front-line role in the campaign to attack Iraq, but so far the Howard government has stood firm. So how will it deal with another Australian who's reportedly declared government policy against Iraq is dumb and not worth the risk? Well, not so easily, when that opinion comes from a senior analyst in the Office of National Assessments, Andrew Wilkie, and pinned to that is his resignation. The Office of National Assessments gathers and interprets an enormous flow of global intelligence material and briefs the PM accordingly. Andrew Wilkie is a Duntroon graduate, a former soldier, a lieutenant colonel and has dropped a bombshell in the national capital tonight with a stinging criticism of the Howard government's policy on Iraq. He joins me now from Canberra. Andrew Wilkie, is it accurate to describe you as a senior analyst with the Office of National Assessments?'

'Yes, Kerry.'

'And you were originally seconded to work there from the Army back in '99?'

'That's right, '99 and 2000 I was seconded there as a strategic analyst in the Strategic Analysis Branch.'

'And the Office of National Assessments more recently, have you been privy to top-level intelligence on areas like terrorism issues and Afghanistan and Iraq?'

'Over the last 15 months or so I've been working [on] global terrorism and transnational issues. Because I'm one of the very small number of ex-military people in the Office, I keep across potential military problems and am called in to work in the National Intelligence Watch Office when those crises blow up. Hence I've worked on Afghanistan, Kosovo and I was on stand-by to work on Iraq.'

'Why have you resigned?'

'Kerry, war must obviously be justified and it must obviously be the option of last resort. I'm not satisfied that in this case it is either justified or it's been viewed as the option of last resort.'

'Was there a particular moment that pushed you over the edge on this decision, I mean it is a big decision. You've walked away on a career.'

'It's the biggest decision I think I've ever made in my life. Frankly I don't know what tomorrow will bring for me. Was there a particular point in time? No, it's been accumulating over many, many weeks, if not months. Although there have been some particular incidents which stick in my mind as incidents which annoyed me very much at the time. For example, when Colin Powell presented evidence to the Security Council some weeks ago now about links between al Qaida and Iraq, and as far as I'm aware there was no hard evidence and there is still no hard evidence that there is any active co-operation between Iraq and al Qaida.'

'But are you satisfied that you're really in a position to know that, to know that in the face of Colin Powell and all the credibility that he might muster?'

'Yes, we are obviously privy to a substantial flow of intelligence, of hard intelligence from the US. We haven't seen anything to prove that there is a link between the two organisations. And, in fact, if you just approach it from first principles, there's a lot of good reasons why there wouldn't be a link. Unless, of course, Saddam Hussein is pushed into establishing a relationship with al Qaida and that's one of the things that I worry about, if there is an invasion of Iraq that that will be just one of the sorts of forces that could push him towards a closer relationship with al Qaida.'

'You wrote an assessment last September [*sic*] on the humanitarian implications of a war with Iraq. What was the essence of that report?'

'That looked at the broadest range of possible humanitarian implications. It … you'd appreciate that I can't disclose intelligence, [that] particular piece of intelligence on *The 7.30 Report*.'

'Were you disturbed yourself by what you found by the assessments you made?'

'Yes. Yes, I was disturbed during my research when I came to realise what a high likelihood there is of a humanitarian disaster. Now, I offered the judgement at the time, and I would stick by it, that a war is likely to be short and successful, but I also offered the judgement that there's a range of activities that Saddam Hussein could take himself to cause a humanitarian disaster, to overwhelm coalition forces, to cause such an international outcry that the war would be stopped, or possibly even ... to embark on a scorched earth policy. Saddam Hussein is on record during the Iran–Iraq war that, when it looked like Iraq could lose that war, he said he will leave nothing of any value for the invading army. That's how he thinks. That's what's in his mind.'

'By the same token a man capable of those kind of expressions and with what everybody knows about Saddam Hussein, how do you feel about the fact that right now you could well be giving comfort and aid, to use a term, to Saddam Hussein? Are you aware, for instance, that your resignation has already been reported in Iran and one assumes that Saddam Hussein might well use your resignation for his own purposes against Australia, and its position against the United States and Britain?'

'Kerry, you're right. But I don't believe I could stand by any longer and take no action as this coalition marches to war. I think the interests of the ... tens of thousands of people or even more who could be injured, displaced or killed in a war, I think their interests are more important. If my action today and over the next couple of days, if it can make the Australian government rethink its position, and maybe take a more sensible approach to developing its policy on Iraq, I think it's been worthwhile.'

'But in the aftermath of September 11, and the fact that there are now terrorists who no longer care about how many people are killed and in fact some of whom may well have the goal of killing as many people as possible, given that Saddam Hussein is quite likely to have a substantial arsenal of weapons of mass destruction, doesn't that concern you as well in terms of potential threat on humanity?'

'Kerry, yes, it does concern me. But I am not saying that we walk away from Iraq. What I'm saying is, and all I am saying, is war must be the last resort and that, before we decide to go to war, we must explore all of the other options at our disposal to disarm him. For example, to improve the inspections, the inspections up until now really haven't been satisfactory. They need to be given more time, more resources and more inspectors. The sanctions could be re-engineered in such a way that more aid can come to people in Iraq who need it and industries such as the oil industry can be rebuilt. So more wealth can come back. I think they're the sorts of approaches we should be taking at the moment in the hope of eventually doing away with this threat.'

'Very briefly, Kim Jones, the Director-General of the Office of National Assessments has issued a brief statement. He says, apart from deeply regretting your actions, he says that you've been a member of the Transnational Issues Branch, [have] been working mostly on illegal immigration and that your work … you were not responsible for ONA's coverage of Iraq. In other words, he's playing down your access to Iraqi issues inside ONA. Is that a fair comment?'

'That he's playing it down, yes. He's doing what I would expect him to do. I don't intend to get into an argument with Kim on this show. He's a man I have a huge amount of respect for and one of the most upsetting things for me today was to walk in and to offer my resignation. But I think, in fairness to me, I've been involved in Iraq in many ways over recent months and I've been particularly interested in Iraq over recent months because I'm on standby to go on to the assessment team for the war.'

'Very quickly, one-word answer, is there any political motivation behind your actions?'

'No.'[2]

It was done. Not a very good performance, but good enough to keep me afloat. Two of my concerns had been addressed – first, that too many things could go awry, and second, that a decision to wage war would be wrong when options short of war had not yet been exhausted. What was disappointing was that I'd let O'Brien control the interview at the expense of addressing the important issue that Iraq did not pose a serious enough threat to justify a war. Lesson learned – I needed to be more disciplined from now on when framing my answers.

I remember a great sense of relief at having survived *The 7.30 Report* and I was happy to do a short interview with Catherine McGrath for ABC Radio National and then share a beer with some of the ABC staff. It was a James Boag Premium, a good drop for a public broadcaster I remember thinking. Odd how little things like that will stick in your mind.

It was then that events took another unforeseen turn. Unbeknown to me, the Parliament House press gallery were now camped in the corridor outside the ABC studios. I gathered that they'd been trying to track me down ever since the original Channel Nine news bulletin had screened at 6.00 p.m. As soon as *The 7.30 Report* had begun, they'd presumably made a beeline for the ABC. 'Can you sneak me out another door?' I asked my hosts. 'We can try,' they responded, 'but if we do they'll chase you around Canberra all night until they get their interview. Better to face them now and be done with it.' Good advice, I decided. It was a shame that I had been starting to relax, sure that my day's work was done. I don't think I finished the beer.

I walked out into the corridor into a battery of micro-phones, cameras and bright lights. It seemed as though hundreds of people had gathered, though perhaps there were no more than a couple of dozen journalists and their offsiders in all.

The mob included faces I recognised – well-known journalists – and I was a little intimidated. I knew I needed to take control so I told everyone we should move down the corridor to where it opened up. Out came the scrap of paper with my memory joggers and off I went into my three key points – 'on-message', as my media-savvy niece Caroline would later say. Again it wasn't a great performance, but at least I'd survived.

*

After my resignation the first opportunity to get back on the front foot came the following morning with the 131st voicemail. It was around midday and the call was from the political party the Greens. They were keen for me to speak at tomorrow's anti-war rally, which was timed to coincide with John Howard's address to the National Press Club. The message stopped me in my tracks. I'd never before been to a protest rally, let alone spoken at one, and doing so now risked politicising my case against the war, which I didn't want to do. But I realised, too, that the appearance might be a good, if final, opportunity to voice my concerns again publicly. After all, I'd already used up almost half of the couple of days in the spotlight that Laurie Oakes had predicted for me. There was no point backing off now: I picked up the phone to tell them 'yes.'

By the next morning, however, I wasn't feeling nearly as convinced that my decision to attend the rally was the right one. To get my anti-war message across I was soaking up as much media as I could handle and moving from whistleblower to activist. But I was feeling the pressure and already starting to tire. After all, I was acting virtually alone, with no support, no adviser, nothing. Plus I'd heard that Howard's address had been moved from the Press Club to the Great Hall in Parliament House for fear of protesters disrupting the event. Addressing a protest rally at the front of Parliament House while the Prime Minister spoke inside – this seemed to me an awfully long way from where a conservative boy from the bush and long-time army and intelligence officer should be.

I had an invitation to join Greens senator Bob Brown for a cup of tea before the Parliament House rally. Brown had come to prominence some twenty years earlier for his role in the campaign to save the magnificent Franklin River wilderness area, and since then had secured his position as one of the heroes of the Left, dedicated to environmental responsibility, social justice and grass-roots democracy. His view on the use of force was just as unequivocal – that it is wrong, except in exceptional circumstances.

Deciding whether or not to meet with Brown was another key moment for me in the weeks that followed my resignation from ONA. In that time I stumbled constantly over many small matters, and my performance during some media sessions was downright awful. But I think I handled well enough the genuinely strategic decisions like this one.

That Brown took almost an hour out of his frantic pre-war schedule to chat with me was a powerful gesture of support at the time when I needed it most. Brown, along with fellow Greens senator Kerry Nettle, would go on later that year to make a splash by interrupting George W. Bush during the US President's speech to the Australian Parliament. But for now he was an ordinary person and a new friend who understood better than anyone what I was going through. Brown too had stepped into an abyss to fight for what he believed in, and for his troubles had been shot at, jailed and beaten. In his early days he'd also been concerned at the misuse of the armed forces, the government once having gone so far as to use air force F-111 bombers to conduct reconnaissance missions over the wilderness activists.

For all Brown's support I can still remember the pain in my stomach that seemed to come from nowhere and grow as the rally approached. I was sick with fear at the thought of addressing the rally, and this despite years of public speaking at high school and later in the Army. In fact I was feeling so unwell that I began to worry that I might end up actually vomiting during my speech, an awful prospect in front of hundreds of protesters and the nation's media. I started to take very long deep breaths. It was all I could do.

When the time came, Brown and I headed out to the assembled protesters separately, so as to keep me at arm's length from any party-political agenda. Better safe than sorry, as the saying goes, although the measure seemed rather unnecessary – I wasn't a member of any political party and was, if anything, more inclined to the Labor Party at that time than the Greens.

What I recall about that moment was the magnificent Parliament House building, the beautiful sweeping lawns and Canberra's brilliant early autumn sunshine. People shouldn't be allowed to make wars from places like that, if only because of the way the comfort, the polite meetings over coffee and the civilised international telephone conversations all combine to quarantine the makers of war from the horrors they unleash.

Stepping up to the microphone against the backdrop of armed police officers, my fear and nausea lifted almost instantly with the warmth of the reception from hundreds of like-minded people. I was among friends and the speech I'd been dreading proved much easier to deliver than I could ever have anticipated. I would attend other, much bigger rallies over the following months, and even speak at some of them, but I'll remember forever the people in front of Parliament House on Thursday, 13 March 2003. They inspired me to continue with my campaign against the war.

At about this time Prime Minister Howard was about to stand up at his own microphone in a last-ditch effort to persuade the Press Club, and through it the nation, of the righteousness of his government's course of action. As expected it was a polished and passionate performance. Yet nowhere did he address squarely any of my detailed criticisms of the impending war, so much so that some in the media were moved to criticise the speech as unconvincing, and an opportunity lost for the government. The closest Howard came to responding to my arguments was to emphasise ONA's support for his government's claims and to give some attention to the hitherto barely mentioned issue of the humanitarian situation in Iraq, in particular by mentioning the fate of children, a risky parallel in light of the 'children overboard' scandal of the 2001 election. Howard had to share prime-time news that night with reports of the protest outside. On balance it wasn't a good day for the government.

LIFE ON THE INSIDE

I was a pilot flying an airplane and it just so happened that
where I was flying made what I was doing spying.
—Francis Gary Power, shot down over the USSR

When I first worked at the Office of National Assessments – from January 1999 until October 2000 – I was on secondment from the Australian Defence Force as a Senior Strategic Issues Analyst. For this the Army's human resource organisation had submitted to ONA a shortlist of candidates from which the Head of Strategic Analysis Branch in ONA chose the most suitable. It was a smooth process, involving little more for me than a few long phone calls between Canberra and my home in Queenscliff. I satisfied the selection criteria, which included a requirement for what is called a 'teeth' arms corps Army lieutenant colonel – infantry, armour or artillery – with an appropriate understanding of defence and strategic issues. Although I jumped at the offer to be shortlisted for the job, I must confess that I knew precious little about what it would entail. I suppose I was as much intrigued as anything else, what with my career manager's vague mentions of 'intelligence', 'international issues' and the like. And in any case the job sounded much more worthwhile and interesting than any of the mindless staff jobs being allocated to many of my peers.

My second stint at ONA – from October 2001 until my resignation over Iraq – took a little more work. I'd been employed by the defence contractor Raytheon since being discharged from the Army but was missing intelligence work enough to grab at an opportunity to return to ONA, this time as a civilian. As though it were yesterday, I recall spotting the advertisement in the *Australian* newspaper for a Senior Transnational Issues Analyst, back in Strategic Analysis Branch, and the fondness I felt straightaway for my old job. I remembered how my work at ONA had always seemed much more worthwhile than anything I'd embarked on at Raytheon. Almost immediately I got in touch with the new Branch Head, who was so enthusiastic that I was confident enough to submit only a wisp of an application. Rather than include examples of my published work as requested, I simply noted that around one hundred intelligence assessments I had written or contributed to were in ONA's records.

Once upon a time, a tap on the shoulder was almost the only way a person was recruited to work for an intelligence agency. You can doubtless imagine the scene – it's still played out regularly in the movies: the star is befriended by an unlikely acquaintance who eventually sounds them out for a secret and dangerous mission.

Nowadays more standard processes apply. Enter 'CIA recruitment' or 'UK SIS recruitment' into a search engine and consider the employment criteria. The Australian Secret Intelligence Service (ASIS) site advises that they are looking for people 'able to take calculated risks.'[1] That makes sense, although this new-fangled recruiting drives some of the old salts to distraction – 'Being a spy was never meant to be like this!'

There's no doubt that certain types of kooks are attracted to intelligence work, although they are weeded out early. You know the sort, the ones who think they're James Bond and have piles of *Soldier of Fortune* magazines stacked under their bed. From what I've seen, those who are left include just about every personality type imaginable. The only constants I could see were that just about all of my former colleagues were smart, stable and trustworthy when it counted. Some were quirky, even genuinely eccentric, but it must be remembered that spying on people and supporting a dishonest government is not like selling vacuum cleaners. In any case, they were as good a bunch of people as I've ever worked with, perhaps even more so than in my Army days.

For a long time there was probably some substance to concerns in the US, the UK and Australia that the intelligence agencies were bastions of conservatism populated by mindless apparatchiks. There is still an element of this, especially at the more senior levels where the governments skew the appointments to their liking, and where the up-and-coming are sharp enough to anticipate the drift of the political currents. In Australia the upper echelons of ASIS are still very obviously committed to the monarchy. In fact you'd be hard pressed to find a better collection of official portraits anywhere than that found hanging in the Canberra offices of Australia's overseas spy agency.

More broadly, though, the intelligence services are slowly coming to better reflect mainstream society. In the Australian intelligence community, the personal feelings of the intelligence officers towards the impending war in Iraq generally reflected the spread, if not the exact proportion, of views on the issue throughout the broader Australian society – everything from strong support for the war and the government through to utter disgust. That much was clear to me before the Iraq war. Of course since then we've seen the many leaks and public statements from serving and retired intelligence officers in the US and the UK, which suggests strongly that a similar spread of views existed in America and Britain.

Some credit for this cultural shift must surely go to the relatively recent decision to recruit most intelligence officers in the US, the UK and Australia in a manner more consistent with standard public-service procedures – selection criteria are set, advertisements appear in the newspapers and online, and applications are lodged. Any other method would be unsuitable for recruiting the very large numbers of intelligence officers required to sustain the enormous intelligence machines of the three countries.

Yet it's not entirely accurate to say that those mysterious taps on the shoulder have entirely disappeared. At least a couple of old army acquaintances of mine were singled out as suitable for covert intelligence work in this way. And those on the inside of the intelligence world still occasionally scout for newcomers – for instance, this method is used from time to time when seeking agents for non-official cover operations, especially by the US and the UK.

In general, though, becoming a spook today is much like applying for any professional position. Except of course that the advertisement is headed bluntly with the name of a spy agency and that applicants are advised to expect extraordinarily intrusive inquiries into their past. For some appointments, applicants will even be notified that the role for which they are applying could be dangerous, that it might involve the breaking of other countries' laws, and that a successful application will probably require them to live a lie, even with some of their closest friends.

What is also unsettling for some aspiring American, British and Australian intelligence officers is the process of being security cleared. The three allies have different degrees of clearance for different roles, but all three enforce a common set of requirements for all personnel working specifically within their intelligence communities.

When I say that all employees within the intelligence community are security cleared, I include in this literally everyone and anyone with any reason whatsoever to enter and move about unescorted in the agencies' secure facilities. Even the cleaners and cafeteria staff are checked out. Absolutely all employees must be cleared to work in an environment where Top Secret material is handled.

The security clearance of those working in the intelligence agencies to the Top Secret level is taken to what's called the 'positively vetted' (PV) stage. This involves an investigation that is about as intrusive as you can imagine and which can take dedicated case officers weeks, sometimes months to complete, at the cost of many tens of thousands of dollars. The matters to be scrutinised are exhaustive. For example, every home address, every country visited, every school attended, every club and society associated with and every substantial financial transaction made is thoroughly investigated. Nor does the investigation stop with the applicant; even current and past partners are investigated, as well as parents and other relations. The aim is to be able to account for applicants' bona fides with absolute certainty.

Eccentricities are permissible, including some that most people would assume to be cause for rejection. One colleague in ONA obtained her clearance although she had once been arrested during a protest at the old US–Australia Joint Defence Facility at Nurrungar in the South Australian desert. But woe betide any applicant caught trying to sneak through an omission or dishonest claim: any such indiscretion, no matter how minor, is cause for instant rejection.

Top Secret is the highest national security category in all three countries, exceeded only by additional specific codewords that are applied from time to time to flag and restrict access further to especially sensitive intelligence. For instance, a piece of very sensitive intelligence such as the Russian President's private views on a sensitive matter such as Chechnya, supplied to the CIA or to the UK's Secret Intelligence Service (SIS) by a senior Russian bureaucrat, would almost certainly be graded Top Secret. It might even be given another caveat, probably a random word, perhaps something quirky and apparently unrelated, if the source provided a specific stream of reporting as part of an ongoing intelligence collection operation. Needless to say, this is a fictitious example. A curious footnote to all of this is that the politicians who see and use the same classified material are not security cleared. Nor are their offices protected to the same degree as those of the intelligence agencies.

To all appearances, the positive vetting process works pretty well – well enough, certainly, to have detected undercover foreign intelligence operatives trying to win employment with ONA. China in particular is inclined to attempt such infiltration in Australia, as well as in the US and the UK.

As part of the Top Secret PV process, prospective intelligence officers are run through a battery of psychological tests. Although many of these are of the standard kind, some are tailored very carefully to match the peculiar demands of specific intelligence agencies. Assessment agencies like the CIA and the

UK's Defence Intelligence Staff (DIS) include testing to determine analytical skills, while the agencies that collect 'humint' – on-the-ground information provided by human sources – are more interested in interpersonal skills as well as stability and decision-making under pressure. Again this process seems to work well, although there have occasionally been obvious exceptions, such as the two Australians bundled out of Australia's Defence Intelligence Organisation (DIO) in recent years – Jean-Phillipe Wispelaere for trying to sell imint (imagery intelligence) to a foreign government, and Simon Lappas for passing intelligence material to his girlfriend.

What awaits applicants who finally make it through the selection minefield can vary greatly. High-end assessment organisations such as ONA recruit subject-matter experts who require little in the way of additional expertise. This is a great strength for such agencies, as each analyst has already proven themselves more than capable in their area. The only downside may be occasional preconceptions about that area of expertise and a lack of good old-fashioned intelligence training. These analysts, of whom I was one, are responsible for geographic areas, e.g. Malaysia, or thematic areas, e.g. Border Security. The other, larger assessors, such as the CIA, DIS and DIO, recruit large numbers of graduates annually, all of whom are put through structured analyst training. This can foster an admirable intelligence culture in such organisations, though it sometimes also leads, in my view, to inexperienced people being immersed in complex issues they are not yet competent to assess.

Intelligence analysts chiefly prepare written and oral assessments on their area of expertise. These are not policy recommendations, but explanations of current events and consideration of possible future developments. They take many forms. In ONA, for example, the main streams of reporting are one- to two-page Watch Reports on current issues, equally brief but more forward-looking Current Assessments, and very occasional and much longer strategic-level National Assessments. All are rigidly capped in length and written in simple terms for the benefit of the non-experts who will read them; often only the most basic explanation of the issue at hand is provided. Adding to the pressure to condense was John Howard's personal direction that ONA's reports be produced in a larger 13-point script so that they would be easier for him to read.

At weekly meetings, the senior management of ONA plan in detail which reports will be prepared, when and by whom. Only unexpected events or unfolding crises can normally override this schedule, most likely in the form of a call for a Watch Report. Once tasked, analysts develop their assessments to a polished draft stage. Each analyst has two computer terminals on their desk to help them with this – one for handling material to Top Secret Codeword-level, the other an ordinary system linked to the worldwide web. The classified machine is a treasure trove, providing ready access to humint, intercepted communications and imagery, and diplomatic cables, as well as to much of the output of most of the American, Australian, British and Canadian intelligence agencies. Analysts will sometimes also consult personally with numerous people outside ONA, including diplomats and intelligence officers posted overseas. All of this can be done easily and quickly via the broad range of secure telephone, email and cable communications systems interconnecting the intelligence agencies and linking them with the diplomatic community.

All of ONA's draft assessments are subjected to a rigorous editing and clearance process. The relevant Branch Head, the

Deputy Director-General and the Director-General all review the draft in detail, and other intelligence agencies as well as relevant policy departments such as Foreign Affairs are often invited to comment. The Director-General's role is particularly significant, going well beyond simply authorising the release of assessments. He personally adjudicates who will write what and when, and he edits in detail the final draft, even to the point of literally standing behind an analyst and supervising the detail and shape of the final version.

Some agencies have recently adopted the military practice of establishing teams that consider and report on issues in a more free-ranging manner, from the point of view of adversaries. These groups, sometimes called 'Red Teams', are powerful tools that seek to break out of the kind of box that stifled effective forewarning of September 11. The CIA established such a team to try to anticipate how Saddam would react to being attacked, and still maintains a team to consider Osama bin Laden's latest thinking. I found the Iraq team's work a very useful tool for understanding some of the more frightening but credible possible outcomes of an invasion of Iraq.

A well-considered intelligence assessment developed over many weeks is easy-street for the relevant analyst or analysts. More difficult is the crisis assessment routinely worked up from scratch in only a few hours at any time of the day or night. These are high-pressure jobs because there is never enough information available to be sure of everything, yet the document produced will likely make an important contribution to the government's decision-making.

Each of the US, UK and Australian assessment agencies has developed mechanisms for handling both short-term and ongoing crises, everything from duty officer and alert systems to recall registers and elaborate operations rooms. I did my penance in such facilities, both at ONA in the National Intelligence Watch Office during the Kosovo and Afghanistan wars, and in the Department of Foreign Affairs and Trade Crisis Centre during the East Timor crisis. Kosovo in particular was a gruelling undertaking – six weeks straight, working seven days a week as part of a two- or three-person shift, with a daily start time that varied between 1.00 a.m. and 5.00 a.m., so that the Prime Minister and the Foreign Minister could have an ONA Watch Report when they started work each day. I didn't begrudge the work, because supporting my country's national security effort in this way seemed to me to be such a worthwhile endeavour. And besides, it was still a long while before I would come to understand just how little Howard and Alexander Downer care about crises of this kind beyond how they affect their immediate political fortunes.

In 2002 I experienced the entire selection process for covert intelligence work, when I decided to apply to work for ASIS. I'd worked closely with the organisation on a number of issues and was impressed by its culture of professionalism. I was very conscious, too, of the better long-term career prospects offered by ASIS when compared with the ONA practice of turning over most staff after one or two contract terms – no more than five or six years for most analysts and their managers. As it turned out, I was knocked out of the ASIS selection process at the final stage, an unsurprising outcome given the brilliant young multilingual applicants I'd encountered along the way. Upon reflection it was probably for the best; at the age of 41 I was a little too old to start a new career competitively with ASIS almost from scratch.

ASIS trains the collectors of humint, and the training is tough yards by any standard. For a start it's long, about five months for the initial Australian course. It's also secretive, with new recruits required to start obfuscating about their new job and its associated absences even before they've headed off to commence their initial training. And of course it's isolated, in surroundings with all the comforts of a three- or four-star resort but nevertheless quarantined from the outside world by countryside, high fences and the heavy shroud of secrecy.

Yet it's also interesting for the trainees, already screened ever so carefully for their suitability for such quirky days in the office. They receive everything from lessons in the psychology of influencing people to mundane training for cover jobs such as diplomatic postings, and spend hours practising their new skills in elaborate training facilities encompassing mock scenes – everything from streets to bars and hotel rooms. Some of it's exciting, especially learning how to cope if things turn nasty, whether by spending sessions at the firing range or by enduring long hours of none-too-gentle interrogation training.

When their teachers think they're ready, it's into town to try out some of their new skills. A trainee might be taken to the local café strip and, without any prior warning, be directed to persuade a particular stranger to do something out of the ordinary. Such a scene was in fact played out quite accurately in the movie *Spy Game*, in which a CIA trainer, played by Robert Redford, gives his trainee, played by Brad Pitt, five minutes to persuade an elderly stranger to allow him entry to her Parisian apartment and to stand at the open window with a cup of tea in her hand. Of course in pure Hollywood style Pitt achieves the remarkably difficult task inside the allotted time. He even ends up at the window himself with his own cup of tea. Is there a lesson in all of this? Perhaps to be wary of sharp young strangers asking you to undertake quirky tasks for no apparent reason.

Once trained, the junior intelligence officers are usually posted to their agencies' headquarters to help out in any of a range of low-level roles while they find their feet. This is an important time for the young operatives, not least because it allows them to grow used to living their lie as they settle back into some sort of normal work routine. Only when their managers are confident the young bucks are ready will they be considered for their first posting, normally as a junior diplomat, often to a country for which they might already have the appropriate language skills.

One of the few concessions the junior undercover intelligence officer might be allowed is permission to reveal, tactfully and cautiously, their real line of work to their partner. This is an important step, one taken only if the officer is confident he or she can trust their partner – disastrous of course would be a trail of knowledgeable and disgruntled former lovers, every one a potential leak. But, if handled well, the bringing of a partner into the loop can provide covert intelligence officers with a very useful asset, especially for those officers posted overseas. Partners can be used tactically to further the chance of mission success – they may help to make initial contact with a potential intelligence target at a social function, for example, or help to break the ice after an introduction is made. Some humint collection agencies even run training courses for agents' partners.

Once overseas, the undercover intelligence officers must play out their double role carefully if they are to succeed. Usually the Head of Mission – the Ambassador or High Commissioner – and some of the diplomatic staff are told who the spooks in the post are, though such information is of course withheld from locals on staff such as drivers. Telling diplomats always involves some risk, and certainly it increases the likelihood of an inadvertent leak, but it also helps to smooth out the workplace wrinkles created by the odd hours and diplomatic underperformance of the spooks. The genuine diplomatic staff of the US State Department, the UK Foreign and Commonwealth Office and the Australian Department of Foreign Affairs and Trade are alert to any loose talk and can be counted on to come down heavily on any slip-ups, although this isn't always enough to prevent some dullard from occasionally blurting out, 'Oh, he's not one of us, he's ASIS' at a DFAT social function.

Keeping the identities of the resident intelligence officers secret from the diplomats is close to impossible anyway, if only because the spies tend to come and go continually from what are obviously their lairs. These are generally the no-go areas buried deeply in the most secure part of the building complex, and protected by additional security-coded doors and other safeguards. Behind them are routine office areas, as well as other, more mysterious zones, in particular the vault-like work areas housing the most secure communications equipment and other gear needed to communicate with headquarters and keep the in-country operation ticking over.

All of this I experienced first-hand as I travelled in the course of my intelligence work. Travel we all did for ONA. By the time it was over for me, I'd visited more than a dozen countries, some on several occasions, and dealt with the trifecta of humint-gathering agencies: the CIA, SIS and ASIS.

Preparing for overseas travel was time-consuming, as I invariably seemed to visit out-of-the-way countries. One challenge was lining up dozens of calls with curious foreign officials, some of whom had little time for Australia: several of them told me straight that nowadays we are arrogant and too close to the US. Wherever I travelled, I enjoyed access to senior officials, although in some cases I suspect this was only because of foreign government misunderstanding of ONA's role – on more than one occasion I was introduced grandly, but wildly inaccurately, as the Prime Minister's National Security Adviser!

Once I arrived in a country, ASIS was normally my 'host', although its officers would only accompany me if they were 'declared' (officially known to be ASIS by the host government). If they weren't, the Head of Station might get involved and drive me around while his team of undeclared spies stayed well clear except when we were in their diplomatic hide.

Travelling overseas as a declared intelligence officer, especially into those countries that from an intelligence point of view are relatively hostile, can be an unnerving experience. Memorable was my time in Hanoi in mid-February 2003. It was the time of the global protests against the impending invasion of Iraq – not that I would have risked getting involved in a rally, especially while overseas on duty. Instead I lay back in my hotel room and absorbed the powerful images being broadcast almost constantly on CNN and the BBC.

The reception on the brand-new television set in my room at the Melia Hotel in Hanoi was superb. The newness of the set suggested that it could well have incorporated at least a hidden microphone and possibly even a camera – such are the risks for the travelling foreigner, declared intelligence officer or not. In fact many countries, including even close 'friends' such as Singapore, mount aggressive intelligence collection operations against a broad range of foreign travellers. Some countries even go so far as to try to compromise high-value targets in the hope of blackmailing them later, just as depicted in the movies. The problem is so prevalent that the US, UK and Australian intelligence agencies monitor the matter closely and publish secret reports advising their officers not only which countries to be especially careful in, but even which hotels to avoid. I was not surprised by the coincidence of my travelling companion's room being exactly above my own, suggesting that this particular column of rooms lent itself to elaborate surveillance. She and I were extra-careful in this place not to mention any sensitive work matter above the quietest whisper.

In May 2002 I spent time in Iran researching a broad range of transnational and strategic issues. This wasn't the first time an ONA officer had travelled overtly into the hard-line Islamic state and the initial preparations went smoothly enough. In Australia I was issued a new diplomatic passport – interesting enough given that I was not a diplomat. But then, at the last minute, the process stalled, when it appeared that my visa would be denied by the Iranian authorities. The penny had dropped that I was actually an intelligence officer, from a country closely allied with the US, seeking to trip around the country investigating everything from the Iraqi–Afghan refugee situation to the fundamentalist government's hold on power. Fortunately, in the end the Australian Embassy was able to smooth it over, helped I suspect by the Ambassador, who had once been a senior ONA officer.

That I'd entered another world in Iran was clear enough as soon as my Emirates flight EK 904 touched down that first morning. Lined up along the runway was a pre-revolutionary time capsule of old C-130 Hercules aircraft, Huey helicopters and US-made Iran Air airliners, all apparently still airworthy despite decades of US sanctions. Entering the terminal I had my first brush with officialdom, handing over my passport to a shifty-looking bloke with an exaggerated moustache who peered at me as though I was Satan himself. Outside an almost new Japanese four-wheel-drive car from the Embassy was waiting, surrounded comically by a sea of old Hillman Hunter cars. Long ago the Iranian government had bought from the English manufacturer the rights to mass-produce the quaint little automobile and since then it had manufactured millions of them as the people's car.

Then to the hotel, a relatively fancy place called the Simorgh, where at last I was able to off-load much of the large bundle of US currency I was carrying in lieu of the credit cards that were useless in Iran at that time. Where was the bug, and possibly the camera, located in this room, I wondered? Maybe they were concealed in the television set, as in Hanoi. Whatever the case, this was one place where my notebooks always stayed with me and where work issues were never discussed in our hotel rooms. That I was under surveillance was beyond doubt, not least because I could see the shadow of moving feet at the base of the door of the room across from the elevators every time I came and went. The two goons who escorted me later to the area near the Afghanistan border were certainly not the government protocol officer and driver they claimed to be. For a start, they knew absolutely nothing about protocol or driving but were treated with the greatest deference by all whom we encountered along the way. Nor did the roadblocks slow us down, let alone stop us. Instead we tore through them at breakneck pace in our unmarked, virtually seatbelt-less car, accompanied always by a blaring music tape and a screeching on-board alarm that told us rather unnecessarily that we were speeding.

My travels were rarely as hairy as that road trip in Iran, though they were often equally sobering, bringing home to me the genuine evil that lurks in our world. For instance there were the shocking Palestinian refugee settlements I saw in Jordan. These were so long-established that at first glance they appeared to be ordinary towns and suburbs, but on closer inspection were revealed as places of despair crammed with people with neither a country to call their own nor any hope for the future. Or in Pakistan the Christian church in Islamabad that only a few weeks before had been attacked by terrorists throwing hand grenades, killing an American diplomat's partner. Or the medical clinic in Taxila, Pakistan that soon after my visit was attacked by terrorists, killing scores of people. And there was the surreal meeting with the spooky Brigadier from the Inter-Services Intelligence Directorate who made my skin crawl – his was the same outfit used for years by the CIA as its gateway to Afghanistan, and the intermediary by which it lent support to a renegade named Osama bin Laden.

It wasn't all grim, though, because for every appalling insight into humanity's flaws there was somewhere else at least one wonderful glimpse of good deeds being done and the magnificent diversity of our world. There were the tireless International Organisation for Migration workers in Jakarta, who care for the hundreds of asylum seekers marooned in the archipelago by Australia's disregard for its obligations as a signatory to the Refugee Convention. Or, in eastern Iran in the city of Mashad, the American aid workers who battle daily the official anti-US bias as they strive to bring decent health care to impoverished people. In Tehran there was the extraordinary Grand Bazaar where I spent hours one day drinking gallons of tea as I negotiated the purchase of a striking silk rug from quite possibly the most animated rug salesmen anywhere in the world. And in Colombo there was the sense of hope that somehow peace might flourish, despite the years of terrible civil war.

All of which is an awfully long way from the routine of an intelligence officer back home where, between crises at least, the daily grind is not dissimilar from the civil service mainstream –

in the office wearing a suit by 8.00 a.m. or so, gone by 6.00 or maybe 7.00 most evenings, days filled with co-ordination meetings and round-table discussions.

Some details, of course, were always quite different from the rest of the public service. Anyone who cares to look can see that access to the ONA building in Canberra is carefully regulated. The drab, four-storey, single-basement building is ringed by closed-circuit cameras and has bollards and concrete planter boxes positioned to prevent a vehicle bomb from getting too close, at least to the front of the building – presumably ASIO has determined that terrorists would not be smart enough to consider driving their truck-bomb across the grass to the side or rear of the well-signposted building! Then there are the glare lights pointing outwards to warn staff and others when to stay clear of the building, the same ones that dazzled Oakes and his crew on the afternoon when I resigned from ONA. The main entry itself is a series of curious tubes made out of a strong, clear material like perspex. Anyone wanting to enter the building needs to activate one of the tubes with their magnetic proximity card, step in only to have the tube shut behind them, wait, and then step out after the far side of the mechanism has opened. Each tube is big enough for only one person, while a sensor in the floor checks against other criteria. As you would expect, the inside of the building is protected by numerous additional systems, such as motion detectors, palm readers, security-coded doors and the like, none of which it would be appropriate to discuss in any detail here.

Because the whole building is so effectively sealed, and because every employee is security-cleared to Top Secret PV, the daily routine inside is surprisingly relaxed from a security perspective. It's not uncommon to overhear extraordinary things as you walk the corridors, or for desks to be littered all day with highly sensitive material, or for computer monitors to be flickering constantly with secret words and pictures. In ONA a great deal of material, including all of ONA's assessments, circulates routinely among most staff for their information. Friends are always talking among themselves about the big issues and whatever else they might be working on. Against this backdrop the compartmentalisation of intelligence material along need-to-know lines tends to break down. Certainly very little material ends up withheld from the senior analysts who work on the broader issues and deal routinely with other analysts.

Life after hours poses challenges even for declared intelligence officers. They need to be careful not to talk about the substance of their work, even to partners and close friends. In fact, especially not to partners and close friends, as these are exactly the types of people targeted by foreign intelligence services sniffing around for secrets. The declared intelligence officers must also maintain their personal circumstances to a standard sure not to compromise their security clearance – marching in anti-war rallies, for instance, is frowned upon, although this didn't stop at least one colleague from attending a number of these after my resignation. Great care has always to be taken with approaches from those interested in the intelligence community, whether they be foreign intelligence officers or, these days, representatives of the media.

In fact, so concerned about public disclosures has the Australian government now become that, upon resignation, ONA officers must declare that they will never speak to the media and always seek clearance before publishing any material whatsoever, forever. These new measures – apparently an attempt to prevent another Wilkie incident – strike me as rather naive.

No government, no matter how dishonest and insecure, will ever find a way to legislate against people determined to speak out for what they believe in.

THE WORLD OF
INTELLIGENCE

You will know the truth, and the truth will set you free.
—John 8:31–32, displayed at CIA headquarters

Members of the intelligence world are called 'spooks' for good reason. Theirs is necessarily another, secret world where very few people go. With secrecy comes naivety among outsiders. Even now, in the wake of unprecedented media scrutiny of the Iraq war, not much is known publicly about the work done by the intelligence services.

It hardly needs saying that this work is far less glamorous than anything depicted by Hollywood. Take, for instance, ONA's National Intelligence Watch Office (NIWO). If you were to visit the NIWO very early one morning, you might see two sleepy-looking people scanning computer screens of data: maps, satellite photographs, diplomatic cables, reports from the field filed an hour or two earlier.

If there is drama here, it comes from the implications of the work, not the task itself. When the Office is activated, its staff work through the night, their task to write a Watch Report on an unfolding crisis somewhere in the world – be it Kosovo or East Timor, Afghanistan or Iraq. Running no more than a page or two in length, the report will be read by the Prime Minister and the Foreign Minister first thing that morning and will provide a basis for their decision-making.

The National Intelligence Watch Office is one of the end-points of a highly complex apparatus, a web of people and surveillance technology that extends over the globe. In Australia, around two thousand people are employed in the intelligence world. The material that converges on the National Intelligence Watch Office is the product of all of these people's diverse labours, which collectively make up an elaborate 'intelligence cycle' that begins with the tasking of relevant agencies, followed by the collection of raw intelligence, the processing and analysis of that material, and finally its distribution to relevant parties, whether they be political or military leaders or other intelligence agencies.

The Office of National Assessments co-ordinates Australia's foreign intelligence effort. To that end it monitors all noteworthy developments in the international arena and periodically works up or revises the National Foreign Intelligence Assessment Priorities (NFIAP) in draft for approval by the National Security Committee of Cabinet (NSC). The NFIAP is a classified document, one that in as little as a page or two illustrates starkly by inclusion what is important to Australia, and by omission what is not.

Interestingly, there was no NFIAP entry for terrorism until September 11, other than the general category 'Threats to Australians Overseas'. This helps to explain why, although it seems unbelievable in retrospect, Australia's senior intelligence agency failed to keep even one full-time terrorism analyst on its books before that terrible day, and why, like the US and the UK, it had no clear warning of September 11. Interesting too is that under John Howard 'Maritime People-Smuggling to Australia' was included in the NFIAPs at the highest level – an irrelevant category from a national security point of view but priceless politically.

ONA's co-ordination work doesn't end with the NFIAPs. Its next task is to turn the government's approved priorities into specific National Intelligence Collection Requirements (NICR). These too are highly sensitive documents, for it is within them that detailed requirements for intelligence are assigned to specific collection agencies. For instance, the NICR on terrorism includes specific requirements for collection agencies to report on any links between foreign governments and the broad Islamic extremist network linked to al Qaida. So too the NICR on Iraq spelled out in detail all that needed to be collected for the threat posed by Iraq to be assessed accurately.

The Director-General of ONA is Australia's most senior intelligence figure. In the US that honour goes to the Director of the CIA who, by legislation, is also the principal intelligence adviser to the President and the head of the US intelligence community. He is responsible for directing and co-ordinating the US's foreign intelligence effort, according to the US equivalents of Australia's NFIAPs and NICRs, such as Presidential Decision Directives.

The senior British spook is the Chairman of the Joint Intelligence Committee (JIC) in the Cabinet Office. Like ONA, the Joint Intelligence Committee spends a great deal of time considering the thinking in Washington and would certainly have continued to do this in the lead-up to the Iraq war, so much so that there are undoubtedly now dozens of 'TOP SECRET JIC UK EYES ONLY' papers on US matters cluttering up safes around London.

When the national intelligence priorities are set, and the collection requirements assigned, the work of gathering raw intelligence begins. Such information takes many forms, including human intelligence (humint), signals intelligence (sigint) and imagery intelligence (imint).

Humint, as the name suggests, is intelligence collected on the ground by operatives, sometimes by penetrating an area or facility to collect information directly, though more often by establishing relationships with others who are encouraged to do the real dirty work.

Such work can often be rather routine. The spies don't parachute onto rooftops in the dead of night or drop into rooms suspended by a thin wire. It is more likely that they will spend their days 'schmoozing', alert to the human emotions that make people vulnerable to cultivation as sources of sensitive information – greed, financial difficulty, lust, revenge, disillusionment; all these and more are exploited to motivate a contact to betray his or her country. Routine or not, though, such operations can be dangerous, both for the operatives on the ground and the people they deal with, especially when it comes to the tricky job of actually handing over information. Spying and treason are serious offences, still punishable by death in some countries. The spine-chilling midnight rendezvous under a damp bridge is not out of the question for the spies at work in the field.

Handling the main foreign humint mission for the US is the Directorate of Operations in the CIA. In the UK the job rests with the Secret Intelligence Service (SIS); in Australia with the Australian Secret Intelligence Service (ASIS). All hide agents under diplomatic cover, for instance a Third Secretary (Trade) in the US Embassy in Paris *could* be an undercover junior CIA officer, while the Counsellor (Political) in the British High Commission in Islamabad *might* be the SIS Head of Station. Of course, these are fictitious examples.

The US and the UK, and other countries too, place some operatives in foreign countries under non-official cover; employed perhaps as expatriate businesspeople or aid workers. These can be especially valuable assets, not least because they are much less easily detected than are those spooks placed in the embassies (all diplomatic employees are regarded as potential spies). On the downside, they operate without any diplomatic protection, and to establish and maintain their cover can be very expensive. In 2003 the CIA programme in this area received a great deal of unwanted publicity when the Bush administration outed Joe Wilson's wife, apparently a business analyst but in reality a CIA agent, in retribution for Wilson's speaking out over the Niger/Iraqi WMD story (something I'll address in more detail elsewhere).

Sigint is derived from the interception of virtually any kind of electronic signal. It includes communications intelligence (comint) and other sources of electronic intelligence (elint). Elint in turn falls into several sub-categories, including radar transmissions, as well as instrumentation signals such as telemetry from missile tests and data from space vehicles. Although it's also collected by other organisations, in particular by the military, the leading sigint agency in the US is the National Security Agency (NSA), in the UK the Government Communications Headquarters (GCHQ) and in Australia the Defence Signals Directorate (DSD).

Most US, UK and Australian sigint is collected by US collection systems. These have the capacity to detect and intercept

52

a range of broadcast transmissions. Land-lines and under-sea cables are normally immune from such attacks, although even under-sea cables have been physically tapped into by some countries over the years during elaborate submarine operations.

The collection systems trawl for information and transmit their catch back to the network of stations operated by sigint alliance partners Australia, Canada, New Zealand, the UK and the US. From there, powerful computers help to route and process the captured information. Meanwhile linguists across the five countries push headsets to their ears as they labour to translate the material into English. Often they'll add a few notes about the source of the intercept and its context. Always they'll slap on an appropriate security classification to help safeguard the precious product – sometimes 'CONFIDENTIAL' if it has been very heavily sanitised for wide distribution, more often 'SECRET CODEWORD' or 'TOP SECRET CODEWORD' to reflect the possible risk to national security should the material ever be compromised. Additional code words are also used routinely to alert the recipient if the intercept is especially sensitive, for example a foreign leader's personal communications, or if it records a telephone conversation concerning a most important subject.

The February 2004 revelation by former British cabinet minister Clare Short that sensitive United Nations communications were intercepted during the lead-up to the Iraq war provided a dramatic insight into the world of sigint. At the time I stayed at arm's length from the matter, although asked often by journalists whether I would substantiate Short's claim. Responding to it, Tony Blair and others offered clumsy denials. In turn, Richard Butler and Hans Blix confirmed that they had been spied on. The cat was out of the bag.

Short was correct in saying that there was a deliberate and official campaign to eavesdrop on the most sensitive United Nations communications during the lead-up to war. No doubt many people assumed that this was the case – they may even have viewed such spying as an unfortunate necessity. Intelligence services are intended to give their country the edge over those countries and groups that seek to compete with and threaten it. Of course this includes many countries who are members of the United Nations, arguably making their UN missions fair game for their adversaries' intelligence services. But sensibly and ethically this policy should not extend to the higher echelons of the United Nations itself. The UN is a special case; it is a body that represents the community of nations. For this reason, the independence of the Secretary-General and his first report officers should be inviolable – and it would be if no individual country thought it was superior to the community of nations' honest broker. The US wanted a war, and the last thing it had patience for was the UN getting in the way. In essence the UN had become part of the problem and it was monitored and assessed with almost as much vigour as was Iraq itself.

Imint comprises the many types of images recorded for intelligence purposes. Specialised organisations, which train experts in particular tradecrafts, take lead responsibility for gathering these images, although numerous agencies contribute material. In the US the National Geospatial-Intelligence Agency (NGA) now does the job, in the UK the Defence Geographic and Imagery Intelligence Agency (DGIA) and in Australia the Defence Imagery and Geospatial Organisation (DIGO).

As with sigint, the collection of imint relies heavily on systems operated by the US. These encompass a broad range of capabilities. Some, for instance, are equipped with electro-optical sensors to collect imagery in the visual range. This is a powerful capability that allows analysts and decision-makers literally to peer down on almost any place on the globe. Other capabilities include access to commercially sourced imagery.

The imagery shown by Colin Powell to the UN Security Council on 5 February 2003 was electro-optical, as was much of the imagery included in the British dossier of September 2002 on Iraq and WMD. These shots were good enough for me and others at ONA to identify easily and quickly Powell's supposed WMD decontamination trucks as mere water tankers, possibly fire trucks.

All of the raw intelligence is gathered up greedily by the assessment agencies and rolled into the mix with whatever other information their subject matter experts can lay their hands on to finalise their analysis and prepare their assessments. No source is spared – all forms of intelligence, defence reporting, mass media including foreign media, books and journals, academic sources, personal contacts, the internet and more are utilised. Routine diplomatic reporting in particular is a vital input, especially from places where covert operations have not been established or are not feasible. Thus, before the 2003 invasion of Iraq, Australian officials travelled repeatedly to Baghdad as part of routine diplomatic responsibilities. But, while in Iraq, they also took the opportunity to make broader observations and inquiries which formed the basis of reports that were transmitted back to Australia by secret diplomatic cable and added to the intelligence database.

Much of the classified material going into the assessment agencies travels electronically via the Top Secret Codeword-rated computer network that links all Australian, Canadian, UK and US intelligence agencies. Only a little remains hard copy, most often the occasional document not worth the effort of transferring to the network. But there are also those documents in need of special handling, not to be disclosed by ONA to other intelligence officials from Australia and overseas.

In the US, non-military intelligence assessments are produced by three organisations: the National Intelligence Council produces long-term estimates; the CIA's Directorate of Intelligence (home to Tom Clancy's Jack Ryan) prepares a broad range of political, military and economic assessments, including National Intelligence Estimates (NIE) such as the one prepared hastily in late 2002 as a primer for the US Congress vote on Iraq; while the State Department's Bureau of Intelligence and Research (INR) provides intelligence support to the Secretary of State and other departmental officials. In the UK intelligence assessment has been centralised under the Joint Intelligence Committee, while in Australia a similar outcome was achieved with the establishment of ONA.

Running in parallel are the extensive military intelligence agencies designed chiefly to provide specialised analysis for the support of war-fighting and other military-oriented operations. In the US the lead agency is the Defense Intelligence Agency (DIA), in the UK the Defence Intelligence Staff (DIS) and in Australia the Defence Intelligence Organisation (DIO), recently in the news for allegedly telling the government only what it wants to hear.

And then there are those agencies concerned principally with domestic issues, namely the Federal Bureau of Investigation (FBI) in the US, the Security Service in the UK, and ASIO in Australia. These are the oddballs of their respective intelligence communities, regarded as spooks but culturally and practically much more inclined to think and behave like cops – unsurprising given their roles as well as their closer relationships with domestic police forces and law enforcement procedures. In Australia this is a particularly unhelpful characteristic, the self-important and sometimes bumbling ASIO – and the Australian Federal Police – sometimes being regarded with some mirth by the broader intelligence community.

Until recently the domestic intelligence agencies were relatively insular in their operations, running virtually stand-alone intelligence cycles and focussing on local threats apparently unrelated to the broader interests of their colleagues. When overlaps did occur, they were rarely the main game, except for the occasional event such as the counter-intelligence operations aimed at foreign intelligence activities. Now that transnational security threats, in particular terrorism, have come to the fore, however, the various organisations have been forced to co-operate much better because their concerns overlap to such an extent. The domestic intelligence agencies are in the spotlight as they play out their lead anti-domestic terrorism roles, and behind them are the broader intelligence communities doing all they can to support them.

Crucial at all stages in the intelligence cycle is the effective sharing of both raw intelligence and completed assessments with allies. For Australia, Canada, the UK and the US, this sharing is a routine process that – when working properly through its electronic connectivity, liaison officers and intelligence exchanges – propels the so-called 'Four Eyes' intelligence relationship into an unprecedented league. No other country or alliance comes close to its power and reach, not even the elaborate intelligence machine that reached out from the Soviet Union during the Cold War. That's not to say that the US-centred behemoth is perfect, of course. Far from it. But it is pretty good and much better than is suggested by some critics who claim the monitoring of Iraq to have been a monumental intelligence failure (something I will address elsewhere in this book).

All of the Four Eyes partners are also members of other intelligence-sharing arrangements. All team with New Zealand for sigint, while the US and UK are key players in the NATO intelligence arrangement. Moreover, all have developed their own special multilateral and bilateral intelligence arrangements. The US, for example, works closely with Israel's Mossad as well as with the intelligence services of a number of countries in the broader Americas, while the UK works closely with colleagues in a number of European countries – a potential boon given the excellent, though narrow, humint and sigint capabilities maintained by France and Germany.

For Australia's part, efforts are made to work as closely as practicable with the intelligence agencies of regional countries. What often gets in the way, however, are the US's strict rules on the sharing of their sigint and imint. Not that this stops the intelligence services of local countries trying ever so hard to establish intelligence-sharing arrangements with Canberra that might win them a degree of access to the American gold, especially by striving to fulfil the constant Australian demands for intelligence on terrorism, people-smugglers and the like.

The day-to-day operations of the Australian intelligence community are conducted along departmental lines – the Attorney-General is responsible for ASIO, the Foreign Minister for ASIS and the Minister for Defence for DIGO, DIO and DSD. ONA reports directly to the Prime Minister. The Prime Minister has overall responsibility, which he exercises through the National Security Committee of Cabinet (NSC), a committee that also includes the Deputy Prime Minister, Treasurer, the Ministers for

Foreign Affairs, Defence and Transport and Regional Services, and the Attorney-General. The chief oversight committee is the Parliamentary Joint Committee on ASIO, ASIS and DSD, though the Joint Standing Committee on Foreign Affairs, Defence and Trade and other ad-hoc committees also play a role from time to time.

Finally there is the somewhat distasteful matter of covert action, such as that undertaken by the CIA's Directorate of Operations: for example, the US$10 million in aid and support the Agency provided to Bashir Gemayel's rightist militia during the civil war in Lebanon, or, even more notoriously, the support given to the Mujahideen and Osama bin Laden in Afghanistan in the 1980s. Not sitting particularly neatly anywhere in the intelligence cycle, this dramatic category of activity is very much at the sharp end, the kind of thing that keeps the real James Bonds of the world busy. It is, by the US government's own definition:

> An operation designed to influence governments, events, organizations, or persons in support of foreign policy in a manner that is not necessarily attributable to the sponsoring power; it may include political, economic, propaganda, or paramilitary operations. This is done at the direction of the President.[1]

As this definition makes clear, almost anything is permissible if it is in US interests and the President is prepared to sign off on it.

In Australia covert paramilitary activities off-shore were banned in 1983 after a botched ASIS training exercise in a Melbourne hotel resulted in smashed architecture, scuffles with senior hotel management and the police being called. Rollback of the blanket prohibition started in secret in 2000 when the National Security Committee of Cabinet agreed to a cabinet submission that limited 'disruption' operations be allowed against people-smuggling syndicates. The policy reversal went further in 2003 when the Australian government agreed to another submission that the carriage of weapons overseas be re-allowed. In Australia's case it's just a matter of time before full paramilitary operations off-shore are again being carried out, if they aren't already taking place.

AN UNNECESSARY WAR

Once they were thick into the planning, Bush couldn't turn back,
of course. That would have made him like the loathed Bill
Clinton – a lot of talk and not much action – not like 'The
Man', as Cheney called his warrior President.
—Maureen Dowd

Washington's real interest in conquering Iraq was surprisingly well understood in London and Canberra. I say 'surprisingly' because Washington was not always frank with its allies during the build-up to the war, so little so that UK and Australian intelligence agencies sometimes needed to treat the US more as a focus of intelligence interest than as a close ally. It is no accident that the National Security Committee of Cabinet in Australia included the US in its National Foreign Intelligence Assessment Priorities.

A reluctance to share information with allies is fine some of the time. US and UK officials presumably aren't fussed about not receiving the Australian intelligence assessments on issues such as border security that shed light on the effectiveness or otherwise of specific Australian government policies. But it is a different matter when vitally important information, such as the latest thinking in the White House, isn't shared about an issue as grave and all-encompassing as the impending invasion of Iraq.

To overcome problems of this kind, the agreement between the US, the UK and Australia (as well as Canada) not to spy on each other is interpreted somewhat loosely. Although Australia is not inclined to spy on the US, it has always been my assumption, one shared by at least some of my former colleagues, that the US spies on Australia. Such operations would be ludicrously easy to run, given that the US designed and operates much of the global spying infrastructure, including the physical links to the Australian systems that store material intended for Australian eyes only.

Australia's corresponding capacity to collect information concerning the US and the UK is far more limited; we must rely instead on the work of diplomats, military staff and intelligence liaison officers who prowl like bottom-feeders for scraps and titbits in the corridors of power in Washington and London. Thanks to such efforts, John Howard (and by his own means Tony Blair) knew before the war began that the US was intent on invading Iraq for many reasons, not only those involving WMD and terrorism. I recall numerous ONA assessments that explored the machinations in Washington and the thinking of George W. Bush and his circle. I'm certain that the UK's Joint Intelligence Committee (JIC) was producing similar assessments. If this knowledge is juxtaposed with the public case for war that was made in London and Canberra, something very interesting is revealed: Blair's and Howard's oft-repeated justifications for going to war were quite hollow. Their statements about WMD and terrorism were made in the full knowledge that such justifications were not the central reasons for the US's actions.

This aspect of Blair's and Howard's behaviour has largely been ignored in the post-invasion recriminations in the UK and Australia; the emphasis instead has been placed on the intelligence services' performance over Iraq specifically, rather than on the broader, and in retrospect more accurate, spying done on the US. Blair and Howard no doubt hope that this will remain the case. It is unsavoury enough that they maintain an intelligence focus on their closest ally; it must be downright alarming to know that what their intelligence agencies told them before the war demolished any remnant of the official case they repeated so assiduously.

ONA understood that a complex mix of reasons, both strategic and domestic, drove the US invasion of Iraq. The war wasn't solely about oil – many reasons swirled around, all eventually converging in March 2003 to create the essential pre-conditions for the conflict. As it was, the spin doctors struggled to keep the crowd up with the game. Imagine the on-air contortions of White House spokesman Ari Fleischer and Downing Street spin doctor Alastair Campbell if they'd been forced to put the case for war honestly.

Oil, of course, was somewhere in the mix of reasons, often rising to the top like a filthy slick on the ocean's surface. Iraq's huge oil lakes, a subterranean reserve second in size only to Saudi Arabia's, are a strategic asset par excellence. (And this assumes no more oil remains to be found in Iraq, an unlikely scenario given the significant tracts of countryside still to be surveyed.) Iraq 'floats on a sea of oil'[1], US Deputy Secretary of Defense Paul Wolfowitz explained, when discussing the need to resolve the issue by force, rather than by diplomatic means (as with North Korea).

Controlling this much oil is an almost unimaginable boon for carbon-hungry America and the cabal of oil company interests associated with the Bush administration. With Iraq comes reliable and cheap access to potential supplies hitherto controlled by a hostile Saddam, paid for in the currency of his choice, and monopolised by the OPEC cartel and foreign companies. The basis of Saddam's real international power was always his oil and how he might regulate its distribution in the future, not any WMD that he might have possessed. If the war had a bottom line, this was it: the US now stands to control an oil reserve of genuinely strategic proportions, one set to become valuable beyond measure over the next fifty years as other oil fields eventually and inevitably run dry.

Superimposed over specifics like oil, however, was a much bigger issue – the US's determination to safeguard and enhance its global ideological, economic and military hegemony. This is the big one: the grand strategy of the US to reign supreme permanently, as espoused by the so-called 'neo-conservatives' and articulated bluntly in September 2002 by the Bush administration in *The National Security Strategy of the United States of America*. In this quest, Iraq was as much a demonstration as a consequence – an almost theatrical performance against a country consequent enough for people to notice, for reasons alarming enough for people to care, on terms lopsided enough to guarantee a crushing demonstration of US military muscle. Or at least that was the idea.

It is possible that some US hawks even judged it better that the war was waged against the tide of international opinion and contrary to international law. Not only was the US's military dominance demonstrated, so too was its belief in the superior morality of its own position. Against this backdrop, Bush's idea that one is either with the US or against it acquires a weird new dimension. No longer is an ally expected simply to co-operate in practical ways. Now one must subscribe to the entire US programme.

There were particular strategic reasons for invading Iraq, notably the practical imperative to shift the US's military and oil-supply centre of gravity out of Saudi Arabia. With its autocratic rule, religious fundamentalism and endemic corruption, the Kingdom had long been a difficult partner for Washington; September 11 and its aftermath brought this tension to a head, to the point where there was open talk in both countries that they were more naturally adversaries than allies. After all, Osama bin Laden is a Saudi and one of his main grievances was the stationing of US forces in the Kingdom; most of the September 11 hijackers were Saudis; and elements in the Saudi government continue to support al Qaida. More broadly, the Kingdom remains a significant financial and scholarly base for the terrorist network. Add to that the inherent instability in the House of Saud, and the US's thinking becomes clear. It knew it had a recipe for eventual disaster. It had to get out.

Underlying this calculation, too, was US consideration for Israel's security. The war was always going to be a good thing for Tel Aviv. Israel stood to lose its main rival, gain all the security benefits of an enhanced, emboldened and more permanent US military presence in the region, and even possibly obtain a share of Iraq's oil and water resources. A good deal, especially given the low likelihood of Saddam having much in the way of WMD, or the missiles to try a repeat of the 1991 Scud attacks, and the fact that there were now much-improved Patriot and other missile systems to intercept such attacks.

That Saddam had almost no ability to project a threat beyond his borders in no way prevented Bush, Blair and Howard from labouring mightily to play up the extent of the danger. No longer was he merely a regional problem, they declared, his WMD arsenal and links to terrorists made him a threat to their own homelands. This was the purest nonsense – by early 2003 Saddam couldn't even control substantial swathes of his own country, or contemplate taking a swipe at his neighbours, let alone mount an attack on more powerful countries further afield.

Iraq took pride of place in the more general scare campaign built up around September 11 and the so-called 'War on Terror'. If the war could be transformed into a genuine national security issue, it had the potential to confer an election-winning advantage on the politicians who waged it. It would distract the rallying US citizenry from the developing difficulties in Afghanistan and their own pressing social, environmental and economic concerns. There was nothing new here, of course – deceitful leaders have focussed attention on national security concerns for domestic political gain as long as anyone can remember.

The scare campaign received a boost from the October 2002 Bali bombing tragedy, especially in Australia. Although I have no doubt that John Howard was genuinely shocked and outraged by the terrorist attack, it also presented him with a potential political windfall, and he proceeded to milk the tragedy for political advantage at every juncture. No angle or opportunity was missed, including his controversial suggestion just before the war that Iraq was actually associated in some way with the terrorist attacks in Indonesia – which of course it wasn't. Months later, at the opening of the Rugby World Cup, he made another spectacularly inappropriate public comment about the Bali tragedy, this time noting the number of its victims who came from rugby-playing countries.

A long list of other considerations – also discussed in ONA – can be added to the mix of reasons that made the US determined to invade. There was the underlying distrust of Iraq – not altogether misplaced, but cultivated by a string of successive administrations. There was the sense of unfinished business remaining from the 1991 Gulf War, even though the Coalition had done everything and more that it was authorised to do under UN Security Council Resolution 678 of November 1990. There was the 1993 Iraqi attempt to assassinate the first President Bush – in ONA's view an unsubstantiated allegation, although one that still made it into the 16 October 2002 Congressional resolution authorising the use of US armed forces against Iraq. There were reckless decision-makers with no understanding of the situation. The list goes on. All were there in the mix of reasons for the war.

In fairness to the US, it must be acknowledged that not all of the reasons for the invasion were unfounded or silly. It's just that the credible reasons always fell well short of a case for a justified war. For instance, the weight of evidence did show that Iraq had a limited WMD programme, but it was not a massive national programme posing such a threat as to warrant a war. And although Iraq provided support for Palestinian terrorist groups, this support was limited and wholly unrelated to the broad extremist network linked to al Qaida. Moreover, the removal of Saddam will probably benefit Iraq eventually. But the idea that the war would start a process that will fundamentally remodel the Middle East for the better did not ring true to me or my colleagues. It assumes not only that the American model is both superior and suitable for transplanting, but also that there is an interest in embracing it. Both assumptions are arguable, the work it seems of people who know a lot about exercising military power but much less about societies unlike their own.

Missing from my list of *reasons* for the war is that grab-bag of important drivers which ONA understood helped to explain the *timing* of the conflict. At the top of the list is September 11, not because it was in any way related directly to Iraq, but because of the terrible sense of vulnerability and anger it stirred up in the US. Overnight Americans felt exposed and scared. They needed to lash out, not just at whomever they were led to believe was responsible for September 11, but at anything and anyone that threatened them. They'd been fought to a stalemate in Korea, defeated in Vietnam and humiliated in Beirut and Somalia. More recently, their embassies and one of their warships had been bombed. September 11 was the final straw. It was time to act.

In an atmosphere such as this, America's virtue was ripe for the plucking by the neo-conservatives associated with the Bush administration, people such as Dick Cheney, Donald Rumsfeld and Paul Wolfowitz, men and women with no compunction about hijacking the September 11 outrages for their own ideological agenda. Their stroke of genius was the so-called 'War on Terror' – a war with no end, no boundaries and no rules. Now the US had the framework for pursuing its goals wherever, whenever and however it chose. Bush saw it this way:

The people who did this act on America, and who may be planning further acts, are evil people. They don't represent an ideology, they don't represent a legitimate political group of people. They're flat evil. That's all they can think about, is evil. And as a nation of good folks, we're going to hunt them down, and we're going to find them, and we will bring them to justice.[2]

The clock was ticking for Iraq. The Bush administration had long had the motive to invade and September 11 gave it the excuse. During a May 2003 interview with *Vanity Fair* magazine, Paul Wolfowitz provided an extraordinary insight into the thinking at Camp David shortly after September 11, extraordinary because the possibility of invading Iraq in response to the attacks was discussed openly, although there was no credible evidence linking Iraq with the terrorist attacks at that or any other time:

> There was a long discussion during the day about what place if any Iraq should have in a counter-terrorist strategy. On the surface of the debate it at least appeared to be about not whether but when. There seemed to be a kind of agreement that yes it should be, but the disagreement was whether it should be in the immediate response or whether you should concentrate simply on Afghanistan first.[3]

This was not the only public evidence of the White House's determination to invade. In *The Price of Loyalty*, former treasury secretary Paul O'Neill evoked the mood that held sway from the very start of Bush's presidency. Speaking to the media, he summed up this mood in the following way:

> From the very beginning, there was a conviction that Saddam Hussein was a bad person and that he needed to go ... From the very first instance, it was about Iraq. It was about what we can do to change this regime ... Day one, these things were laid and sealed.[4]

More recently Richard Clarke, in *Against All Enemies: Inside America's War on Terror*, provided further insights into

Washington's obsession with attacking Iraq, even though all the evidence pointed to al Qaida being responsible for September 11. Describing events in the days immediately following the attacks, Clarke writes:

> Rumsfeld was talking about broadening the objectives of our response and 'getting Iraq.' ... Secretary [of State Colin] Powell pushed back, urging a focus on al Qaida. Relieved to have some support, I thanked Powell and his deputy, Armitage ... 'I thought I was missing something here,' I vented. 'Having been attacked by al Qaida, for us now to go bombing Iraq in response would be like our invading Mexico after the Japanese attacked us at Pearl Harbor.' ... Powell shook his head. 'It's not over yet.' Indeed, it was not. Later in the day, Rumsfeld complained that there were no decent targets for bombing in Afghanistan and that we should consider bombing Iraq, which, he said, had better targets. At first I thought Rumsfeld was joking. But he was serious and the President did not reject out of hand the idea of attacking Iraq. Instead, he noted that what we needed to do with Iraq was to change the Government, not just hit it with more cruise missiles, as Rumsfeld had implied.[5]

Even more recently, veteran journalist Bob Woodward has revealed in his book *Plan of Attack* that Bush ordered a plan be drawn up for the invasion of Iraq within weeks of September 11.

If the events of September 11 were the crucial pre-condition for the Iraq war, it was nevertheless understood in ONA that the 2002 US mid-term congressional election was the essential trigger. By then the so-called 'War on Terror' was barely stumbling along – the Taliban had been toppled and some senior al Qaida figures killed and captured, but Afghanistan was still a security headache, al Qaida had not been crushed, and Osama bin Laden was still at large. Americans were starting to tire of it all and re-focus on the raft of domestic issues the Bush administration seemed least competent to deal with, in particular the economy. Hence, in late August 2002 – a couple of months before the election – the Bush administration decided to re-invigorate the national security issue by dragging the Iraq bogyman out of the closet. On 26 August 2002, in Nashville, Vice-President Dick Cheney told the Veterans of Foreign Wars Convention:

> Simply stated, there is no doubt that Saddam Hussein now has weapons of mass destruction. There is no doubt he is amassing them to use against our friends, against our allies, and against us. And there is no doubt that his aggressive regional ambitions will lead him into future confrontations with his neighbors – confrontations that will involve both the weapons he has today, and the ones he will continue to develop with his oil wealth.

In early September, the story was leaked to the *New York Times* that Saddam was determined to build a nuclear bomb. It was a simple strategy, but it worked and the Republicans did very nicely.

By implication, though, the US was now marching to war. If only for the sake of American credibility and the political survival of the Bush administration, nothing was going to be allowed to stop this march. That Iraq didn't have a massive WMD programme and wasn't co-operating with al Qaida was irrelevant. That there was virtually no international support and that the UN Security Council had refused to endorse the adventure was

beside the point. Certainly the US hoped to obtain more support from the UN than it did; it would have been delighted to
have secured an appropriate Security Council resolution – most
people in the US government are quite sensible, and even George
W. Bush knew the importance of this for Tony Blair. In the end,
though, dealings with the UN became little more than theatrics.
Hang the risks and consequences, the US had locked-and-loaded.
By late 2002 nothing could stop the countdown to war.

Blair and Howard understood this clearly because their intelligence agencies were telling them so – I know this was the case
in Australia and I'm certain the situation was identical in the
UK. In other words it was well understood in 2002 in ONA that
the US would soon invade Iraq – almost certainly by early 2003,
before the heat of the Iraqi high summer made war-fighting too
difficult. US intentions were also clearly signalled by specific
aspects of the build-up of forces in the Gulf region; these were
geared much more towards fighting a war than merely pressur-
ing Iraq to bend to UN demands. For instance, there was the
politically risky stationing of forces in Jordan, as well as the mil-
itarily risky insertion of special forces into Iraq itself.

That ONA – and therefore the senior figures in the
Australian government – understood clearly what was going on
in Washington is evidenced by my recollection of an afternoon
tea meeting in 2002 at the Australian Strategic Policy Institute
(ASPI) in Canberra. At this meeting the members of ONA's
Strategic Analysis Branch, including myself, argued strongly with
the disbelieving ASPI head Hugh White about the inevitability
of the impending war. White was convinced that the US would
not go to war with Iraq, and also made the assessment that Iraq
had a substantial WMD capability. So much for Australia's top
think-tank.

Although Howard had clearly decided by late 2002 to support Bush's war, this decision was not a formal decision of government. Rather it was an understanding of the US's intentions and a determination to support them – at any cost. In this sense, Howard is correct in saying, as he has repeatedly, that no decision was made by the government to support the war until just before the invasion began.

Nevertheless Howard knew what was brewing long before the National Security Committee of Cabinet formally deliberated on the decision to commit Australian troops. ONA's reporting on the US – in accordance with the government's direction – was prolific during the lead-up to hostilities. Moreover, the occasional telephone conversations with Bush, about which Howard boasted publicly, also ensured that the Australian government was well-informed enough to be able to read the situation in Washington.

The government's determination in 2002 to support the war was conveyed to the public, to some degree, by Howard's and Downer's official statements. It was conveyed to the bureaucracy much more strongly, albeit by a process of osmosis. The government's determination was gradually absorbed and diffused into a clear understanding that Australia would participate in the war. ONA knew this by late 2002; the Australian Defence Force had begun to prepare even earlier – as far back as mid-2002, for example, the Special Air Service Regiment in Perth was focussed on the need to be ready for the formal order to deploy troops to Iraq.

Blair and Howard knowingly recycled the US's case for invading Iraq so as to stay in step with Bush. They understood the broader US agenda and were sympathetic to much of it. Both were obviously conditioned by shared history and values.

More particularly, the Blair–Bush deal must be seen in the context of the broader trans-Atlantic, US–UK–Europe security tug of war, while Howard's specific position was part ideological, part egotistical. Ultimately Blair and Howard found themselves driven mostly by their obsession with fostering their countries' relationships with the US at any cost; in practice what this amounted to was ingratiating themselves with Bush by supporting a war which they both had known for a long time was inevitable. Neither seemed to understand the potential consequences of the terrible game they were playing.

It was not a conspiracy between the three leaders, but rather an overlapping of interests. For its own reasons the US took the lead on the WMD/terrorism story. For their own reasons it was convenient for the UK and Australia to tag along. Wolfowitz at one point explained the US government's approach to Iraq as the product of a bureaucratic consensus among the relevant US bodies. On reflection this is only one-third of the whole story, because the official British and Australian cases for war were themselves the product of a consensus with the US, in which the US set the terms. The Big Lie was joined.

THE BIG LIE

The first panacea for a mismanaged nation is inflation of the currency; the second is war. Both bring a temporary prosperity; both bring a permanent ruin. But both are the refuge of political and economic opportunists.

—Ernest Hemingway

The invasion of Iraq was sold on the basis of that country possessing a massive arsenal of WMD and co-operating actively with terrorists. These claims were made in many different ways and have since been radically re-engineered, but the heart of the official case against Iraq made in Washington, London and Canberra was always as follows: Iraq possessed significant quantities of chemical and biological weapons, it was determined to acquire nuclear weapons, and it was consorting with al Qaida.

The September 2002 dossier, *Iraq's Weapons of Mass Destruction: The Assessment of the British Government*, was a key building block for the case, not least because of its timing and scope. The build-up to war was well underway by the time the dossier was released

– the dominant view within ONA by then was that war was inevitable – but never before had such a comprehensive, apparently intelligence-driven case been put publicly. The dossier's main conclusions included the following:

> Iraq has a useable chemical and biological weapons capability, in breach of UNSCR (United Nations Security Council Resolution) 687, which has included recent production of chemical and biological agents;
>
> Iraq continues to work on developing nuclear weapons, in breach of its obligations under the Non-Proliferation Treaty and in breach of UNSCR 687. Uranium has been sought from Africa that has no civil nuclear application in Iraq;
>
> Iraq's military forces are able to use chemical and biological weapons, with command, control and logistical arrangements in place. The Iraqi military are able to deploy these weapons within 45 minutes of a decision to do so.[1]

To many non-experts and some experts alike, the eagerly awaited dossier presented a strong case for war, strengthened further by the unambiguous foreword by Tony Blair himself:

> I believe this issue to be a current and serious threat to the UK national interest ... Saddam Hussein is continuing to develop WMD, and with them the ability to inflict real damage upon the region, and the stability of the world ... It is clear that, despite sanctions, the policy of containment has not worked sufficiently well to prevent Saddam from developing these weapons ... I am in no doubt that the threat is serious and current, that he has made progress on WMD, and that he has to be stopped.[2]

One of the most important US arguments for war was also made at this time, when George W. Bush delivered his 7 October 2002 Cincinnati address. As this was his last opportunity to convince Congress to vote for the possible use of the American military to enforce UN Security Council resolutions, he went in hard, especially on the nuclear and terrorism issues:

> [Iraq] possesses and produces chemical and biological weapons. It is seeking nuclear weapons. It has given shelter and support to terrorism, and practices terror against its own people. The entire world has witnessed Iraq's eleven-year history of defiance, deception and bad faith.
>
> We know that Iraq and the al Qaida terrorist network share a common enemy – the United States of America. We know that Iraq and al Qaida have had high-level contacts that go back a decade. Some al Qaida leaders who fled Afghanistan went to Iraq ... We've learned that Iraq has trained al Qaida members in bomb-making and poisons and deadly gases. And we know that after September the 11th, Saddam Hussein's regime gleefully celebrated the terrorist attacks on America.
>
> The evidence indicates that Iraq is reconstituting its nuclear weapons program. Saddam Hussein has held numerous meetings with Iraqi nuclear scientists, a group he calls his 'nuclear mujahideen' – his nuclear holy warriors. Satellite photographs reveal that Iraq is rebuilding facilities at sites that have been part of its nuclear program in the past. Iraq has attempted to purchase high-strength aluminium tubes and other equipment needed for gas centrifuges, which are used to enrich uranium for nuclear weapons.[3]

Congress was persuaded.

Bush's 28 January 2003 State of the Union address comprised more of the same. Prominent was the claim that, 'The British government has learned that Saddam Hussein recently sought significant quantities of uranium from Africa.'[4]

For his part, John Howard made it quite clear in his 4 February 2003 address to the Australian Parliament that his government endorsed the views being expressed in Washington and London, including those contained in the American and UK reports released on Iraq. He also sought to make clear Iraq's association with the 'War on Terror':

The Australian government knows that Iraq still has chemical and biological weapons and that Iraq wants to develop nuclear weapons.

In hindsight the world has been too trusting – not careful enough in its dealings with the Iraqi President. But the situation is different now. Iraq has not changed – but we have. We now understand, after the event in Bali and those of 11 September 2001, that we are living in a world where unexpected and devastating terrorist attacks on free and open societies can occur in ways that we never before imagined possible.[5]

The following day the US Secretary of State, Colin Powell, made probably the most comprehensive and persuasive case for the invasion of Iraq when he addressed the UN Security Council. The 5 February presentation in New York was a powerful performance by Bush's most credible player, so much so that on one estimate the pro-war sentiment among editorial writers for large US newspapers doubled overnight (rising to three-quarters in favour).

Powell laid out an avalanche of allegations against Iraq. He unveiled an impressive collection of communications intercepts and grainy satellite photographs, along with information from mysterious human sources:

We know from Iraq's past admissions that it has successfully weaponised not only anthrax, but also other biological agents including botulinum toxin, aflatoxin and ricin. But Iraq's research efforts did not stop there.

Saddam Hussein has investigated dozens of biological agents causing diseases ...

Our conservative estimate is that Iraq today has a stockpile of between 100 and 500 tons of chemical weapons agent ...

Saddam Hussein already possesses two out of three key components needed to build a nuclear bomb. He has a cadre of nuclear scientists with the expertise and he has a bomb design.

Since 1998, his efforts to reconstitute his nuclear program have been focussed on acquiring the third and last component: sufficient fissile material to produce a nuclear explosion. To make the fissile material, he needs to develop an ability to enrich uranium. Saddam Hussein is determined to get his hands on a nuclear bomb.

Iraq and terrorism go back decades ... But what I want to bring to your attention today is the potentially much more sinister nexus between Iraq and the al Qaida terrorist network ...[6]

Much more, of course, was said by the main players before the start of the war. Some public statements were quite hysterical, such as Australian Foreign Minister Alexander Downer's 17 February 2003 speech at the Sydney Institute entitled 'The Spread of Nuclear, Chemical and Biological Weapons: Tackling the Greatest Threat to Global Security – The Sum of All Our Fears'. Others were more sensible, such as British Foreign Secretary Jack Straw's 7 March address to the UN Security Council entitled 'We Have To Put Saddam to the Test'. But, whatever their style, all pushed the line that Iraq had to be disarmed because it possessed a substantial arsenal of WMD and was co-operating actively with global terrorists including al Qaida.

The powerful and apparently trustworthy status of these advocates lent great authority to the vast quantity of pro-war material being pushed out of Washington, London and Canberra – regardless of the merit or otherwise of the argument. As O'Brien had asked me on *The 7.30 Report*: 'But are you satisfied that you're really in a position to know that … in the face of Colin Powell and all the credibility that he might muster?' A fair question, even in retrospect.

The official case for war gained credibility in light of Iraq's long history of interest in WMD. Iraq had established WMD programmes decades ago, out of concern for the threats posed to it by Israel and Iran. The chemical weapons programme was initiated in the late 1960s, contracts to purchase Scud missiles were first signed in 1972, the biological weapons programme was underway by the mid-1970s and a nuclear weapons capability was being pursued by the time of the first Gulf War in 1991. Moreover, that Iraq was prepared to use such weapons had been made terribly clear, first during its 1980–88 war with Iran, when large quantities of chemical weapons were used by both countries, and again in 1998 when Iraqi forces used chemical weapons against Kurds in northern Iraq.

All of this seemed to add up to a very weighty case against Iraq, and not one open to dispute. But of course I did want to dispute it. There is no single issue, or shocking secret report, or classified intelligence assessment that I can refer to in order to explain how the Iraq threat was blatantly exaggerated for political purposes. The process was not that dramatic. Rather, the US, UK and Australian governments were guilty of playing out the exaggeration over many months, in sometimes bold, but more often subtle ways.

Most often the deceit lay in the way Washington, London and Canberra deliberately skewed the truth by taking the ambiguity out of the issue. Key intelligence assessment qualifications were frequently dropped and much more definite words put in their place, even though such embellishments had not been offered to the governments by their intelligence agencies. Before we knew it, our political leaders had created a mythical Iraq, one where every factory was up to no good.

Crucially, there were significant intelligence gaps on Iraq. These were consistently filled with sequences of doubtful information based on worst-case assumptions, all of this finely tuned to reinforce the need to invade.

Two of these gaps are especially important: the unaccounted-for pre-1991 Gulf War WMD, and the uncertainty surrounding Iraq's actions between the withdrawal of the UN Special Commission (UNSCOM) in 1998 and the arrival of the UN Monitoring, Verification and Inspection Commission (UNMOVIC) in late 2002.

The US, the UK and Australia all went to a great deal of trouble to highlight that, based on UN assessments, unaccounted-for WMD material included up to 360 tonnes of bulk chemical agent, up to 3000 tonnes of precursor chemicals, enough growth media to produce tens of thousands of litres of biological agent, and over 30,000 special munitions suitable for delivery of chemical and biological agents. However, the continued reference to these figures in the case for war appeared to me to be simply ridiculous, not least because no-one, not even the Iraqis themselves, knew exactly how much chemical and biological agent they'd produced, exactly how much was used during the 1980–88 Iran–Iraq War or exactly how much was destroyed later outside of UNSCOM control.

Reliance on the list of unaccounted-for material was also absurd for another reason. The list failed to account properly for the critical issues of agent purity and degradation over time. Most chemical and biological agents soon break down unless produced to a very high level of purity and then effectively stabilised, but Iraq always had great difficulty achieving high levels of agent purity and it never developed the know-how to stabilise the finished products. Claims to the contrary are simply not substantiated by any hard intelligence. The exception to this, of course, is mustard gas, which can remain potent for many years, but this is a crude agent that must be used in vast quantities and in favourable conditions if it is to be effective as a WMD. The limited quantities identified in the list of agents unaccounted-for do not satisfy this criterion. The 550 shells mentioned by Powell during his address to the UN Security Council on 5 February would, between them, have amounted only to a very limited capability.

This brings me to the second major intelligence gap on Iraq – exactly what Saddam's regime did between the withdrawal of UNSCOM and the arrival of UNMOVIC. In the main, the claims that Iraq had re-commenced production of chemical and biological agents had a simple basis: Iraq had started to rebuild

facilities previously associated in some way with its WMD programme, as well as to build new facilities. Yet these claims were
consistently unsupported by any hard evidence that such facilities were actually producing WMD. In fact the UK's September
2002 dossier sometimes suggests quite the opposite; it refers to
the Tarmiyah chemical research centre but notes that it under-
took research, development and production of chemicals needed
for Iraq's civil industry, commodities that could not be imported
because of the international sanctions.

These oft-repeated claims about so-called 'dual-use' facilities troubled me in the lead-up to the war. In all countries
numerous facilities and materials used for legitimate purposes
are suitable also for production of WMD-related materials – the
US, the UK and Australia have thousands of such facilities.
Accordingly, it was always preposterous that Washington, London
and Canberra made such a fuss over Iraqi dual-use sites and
materials in the absence of any corroborating intelligence. The
reports were sometimes plainly silly. Much, for example, was
made of the Fallujah II chlorine and phenol plant, although
UNMOVIC had found it to be inoperative.

An important consideration here is the technical and practical difficulty of rebuilding, hiding, supplying and operating
chemical and biological facilities on such a scale as to constitute
a genuine national WMD programme. Washington, London and
Canberra fostered the impression that such an undertaking was
not a difficult one for an evil dictator with lots of oil money.
But this is downright misleading. For the Iraqis to rebuild their
WMD programme since 1998, virtually from scratch, would
have been a substantial undertaking. Tellingly, even the US never
perfected the military weaponisation of anthrax, although it
devoted enormous resources to this and it had no need to hide

its WMD programmes – hence in part its decision to end its offensive biological weapons programme and sign the Biological Weapons Convention.

There were also too many blatant inaccuracies and misrepresentations in the case against Iraq made by Bush, Howard and Blair. The UK's September 2002 dossier singled out the Amariyah serum and vaccine plant west of Baghdad as a facility of concern, for example, but the dossier's release was soon followed by reports from journalists who were allowed into the buildings at the plant within hours of the dossier's release and found there empty fridges. Or again, when John Howard spoke in parliament of Iraq having 'form', he disregarded the intelligence advice he was receiving about the state of affairs in Iraq and instead dragged up a string of pre-1991 Gulf War examples, such as the use of chemical weapons against Iran and the Kurds.

On balance the strong, unambiguous language contained in the case for war seemed more the work of salespeople than professional intelligence officers. The claims that the repeated assertions reflected accurately the views of national intelligence agencies are plainly wrong. They were simply too much at odds with the piles of intelligence material I was privy to, including material from the CIA, INR and JIC. In all the material I saw on Iraq, never did I see such a string of unqualified and strong judgements as was contained in the official case for war presented by Bush, Blair and Howard.

The US, UK and Australian intelligence agencies generally produced compromise assessments, which reflected the balance of a broad range of source material and analysts' views. Their output was, and still is, full of terms such as 'probably' and 'could'. In such assessments, contentious issues are either dropped from the document that goes to government or heavily qualified.

Nowhere was this more relevant and obvious than in the material being prepared on the highly uncertain Iraq issue. But this uncertainty was not reflected in the official case for war – and if doubt is not particularly headline-grabbing, its removal nevertheless goes to the heart of the deception over Iraq. I emphasise that the agencies were producing measured assessments and that all it took to distort their work decisively was for politicians and their advisers to omit a few words like 'uncorroborated evidence suggests' and insert a word or two like 'massive'. The result was the creation of an entirely new threat. In essence, the politicians turned uncertainty into certainty.

Bush, Blair and Howard also chose to use the truth selectively, for example by regularly playing up the risk of WMD terrorism but neglecting to point out that the likelihood of such an attack is low. This is an important issue, one worth dwelling on. After all, it was the fantastic official talk about the inevitability of terrorists very soon getting their hands on WMD – in particular al Qaida obtaining these weapons from Iraq – that brought together the disparate threads of the case for war in a very persuasive way. Saddam was not only armed to the teeth with a massive WMD capability, so the pro-war group claimed, but he was in bed with that other arch-villain Osama bin Laden. A transfer of WMD was only a matter of time. What remained unsaid was that all this very alarmist talk was quite at odds with the measured advice contained in the highly classified intelligence assessments being worked up in the US, the UK and Australia on the risk of WMD terrorism.

Before the Iraq war there were few instances of terrorists using chemical or biological weapons. None of these attacks had caused mass destruction. There had been no substantiated instance of terrorists staging a radiological attack. And of course there had been no instance of terrorists detonating a nuclear weapon. The few substantiated examples of such unconventional terrorist attacks – the 1984 poisoning of local restaurant salad bars with salmonella bacteria by an Oregon cult led by the Bhagwan Shree Rajneesh, the botched 1995 sarin gas attack in the Tokyo subway by Japanese cult Aum Shinrikyo and the 2001 anthrax-laced letters in the US – had produced results far smaller in scale than the potential horrors depicted by officials in the lead-up to the Iraq war.

The rarity of WMD terrorism until now is no accident. Most terrorists have not been prepared to cross the psychological barrier associated with WMD. Even terrorists have generally found WMD abhorrent, because even they have a stake in the future and a belief that this is a world worth living in. Moreover, most terrorists have limited political goals best pursued by limited means. They hope to force political change, but at the same time recognise the importance of maintaining or developing community support and limiting to survivable levels the official response to their actions. As nationalists, most terrorists have neither the need nor the desire to attack and terrorise on a broader front, especially when this may have the effect of restricting support from further afield. How all of this is changing, most notably in the case of al Qaida, is an issue that I'll address elsewhere in this chapter.

Serious technical hurdles also help to explain the very limited terrorist interest in WMD. Although simulations and contingency planning understandably tend to focus on worst-case scenarios, the reality is that obtaining, manufacturing, storing, weaponising and dispersing WMD is extremely difficult. Except in the case of so-called 'low-end' agents, access to the ingredients of chemical and biological weapons is generally tightly controlled. The processes to prepare the weapons are difficult, they are often unstable or highly corrosive when manufactured, their dispersal is dependent upon very carefully calibrated measures, and once dispersed they are vulnerable to wind, sunlight, ozone and smog. The unsophisticated, more easily prepared low-end agents are generally only able to cause large numbers of casualties when they are used in very large quantities – tonnes normally, when it comes to chemical agents – or in confined venues that can hold a substantial number of people.

For instance, Aum Shinrikyo had an enormous sum of money at its disposal for development of chemical and biological weapons. It had front companies that allowed it to source appropriate equipment, several members with relevant post-graduate degrees, and an impressive research library. It took years to prepare for its attempts to poison and infect large numbers of people in Japan. In spite of all of these advantages, Aum could neither produce successfully nor disperse effectively the botulinum or anthrax that it was attempting to utilise. Aum sprayed botulinum in Tokyo several times in 1990 and conducted similar activities with anthrax in 1993, but without any known effects because the cult had used a relatively harmless type of anthrax and inefficient aerolisers. Aum's attempts to use a chemical agent are much better known, although they were almost as unsuccessful. Three kilograms of sarin was dispersed in Matsumoto in 1994 and about six kilograms of sarin was dispersed on the Tokyo subway in 1995. Both attacks were launched under good conditions. Thousands of people suffered ill effects, but between them the attacks killed only around 20 people.

The risks are even smaller when it comes to radiological and nuclear devices. Radiological weapons are really no more than bombs designed to spread radiation, usually by using a combination of explosives and some form of radioactive material, most likely something obtained easily such as medical isotopes grabbed from a health-care facility, or low-grade radioactive waste stolen from any one of a large number of relatively insecure depositories around the world – such as the flimsy tin sheds in Australia's Woomera Prohibited Area in South Australia. High-level radioactive material is much more tightly safeguarded. Fortunately, in all probability the effect of such weapons would be far less lethal than is portrayed routinely in the media. In fact, they would probably cause more disruption than destruction – most or all of any casualties would be caused by the explosive blast rather than by the low-level radiation spread by the explosion.

The likelihood of terrorists obtaining a nuclear bomb remains so small as not to warrant much comment. Building an effective nuclear weapon – as opposed to a very low-yield 'fizzer' – is too difficult a task for most countries to accomplish, let alone a terrorist organisation. Moreover, the likelihood of a weapon leaking somehow from a state arsenal is also judged by intelligence agencies to be very low. Paranoid countries like North Korea are hardly going to give away or sell their most precious safeguards against their adversaries, while Russia keeps a better eye on its nuclear weaponry than many commentators give it credit for. I recall clearly from my time in ONA that there was no hard evidence whatsoever to substantiate the urban myth that old Soviet suitcase bombs and the like – known more accurately as special-purpose munitions – had either gone missing or were available for purchase.

In short, conventional weapons are a more attractive proposition for most terrorists. They are more readily available and can be obtained with much less risk of detection. They also pack a punch – the Bali bombing illustrated the power of low explosives. Moreover, September 11 showed dramatically the effectiveness of improvised weapons. By any measure the lethal combination that day of religious fanaticism, innovation, surprise, box-cutters and large aircraft produced horrifyingly effective weapons.

None of this is to dismiss outright the threat of chemical, bacteriological or radiological (CBR) terrorism. The nature of non-state violence is changing. Extremist organisations have emerged who have no stake in the future of this world. The benchmark for the lethal use of terrorist weapons has been raised after September 11, and the know-how to make WMD is becoming more accessible to a wider range of people. And of course the extremist network linked to al Qaida in particular has long been interested in WMD. But none of this translates automatically into Osama bin Laden, or any other terrorist leader for that matter, being able any time soon to make the enormous capability leap from a simple to a sophisticated CBR weapon.

The key term here is WMD – Weapon of Mass Destruction. The definition of 'Mass' is still controversial, perhaps falling somewhere in the thousands of casualties. But whatever the case, the low-end CBR devices most likely to come into the possession of terrorists would not effect this scale of lethal destruction. Hence, for the foreseeable future, terrorists are much more likely to try to kill by using platforms like trucks, boats or aircraft, or more innovative ideas like bushfires, rather than crude CBR devices which are considerably more trouble to obtain and produce similar or inferior results. Unless, of course, the terrorists aim more to terrorise than to kill, as in the case of the 2001 anthrax mail attacks in the US where the beat-up of WMD terrorism that has occurred in recent times plays right into the terrorists' hands.

State-sponsorship of terrorism is a relevant issue here, for such sponsorship could, conceivably, allow terrorists to fast-track their access to a genuine WMD while providing the sponsor with an alternative way of achieving its own foreign policy goals. But, again, before the Iraq war the intelligence agencies assessed the probability of such an occurrence to be very low, in part because of the understandable concern in potential supplier states about the devastating repercussions should their involvement in such a scheme be discovered by the US.

Iraq was no exception to this rule, given its contained WMD programme and its limited relationship with regional terrorist groups. The US, the UK and Australia never collected any hard intelligence to back up their specific and oft-repeated claim that Saddam's regime was actively co-operating with the broad Islamic extremist network associated with al Qaida. It should be recalled, too, that Saddam was a secular dictator intent on eradicating Islamic fundamentalism. Any Iraqi involvement with terrorism was therefore directed at Iran, Syria and exiled opponents, or took the form of support for specific Palestinian groups. Stories to the contrary were all contrived or unsubstantiated, such as the nonsense that September 11 hijacker Mohammad Atta had met with Iraqi intelligence officials.

Before the war, much was made of the Ansar Al-Islam camps in Iraq and in particular their so-called 'poisons factory'. Such camps were indeed legitimate evidence of an ongoing interest in unsophisticated chemical weapons among the broad network linked to al Qaida. In no way, though, did they prove a link between Osama bin Laden and Saddam, simply because all of the known Ansar Al-Islam activity in Iraq was, to use an ONA term, 'in an area outside of Saddam's control'. So many times was the complete disconnection between Iraq and al Qaida emphasised in the official advice to the Australian government – advice shared routinely with the US and the UK governments – that I can still recall it word for word.

Equally unbelievable was the tale that Iraq had tried to purchase thousands of aluminium tubes from a Chinese supplier for use in uranium-enriching gas centrifuges. My first encounter with this issue was late in 2001, during the Australian intelligence community's annual conference on WMD at the ASIS training facility. The topic of WMD was familiar to me by that time. Although not a scientist, I'd become involved in the issue somewhat by accident during 1999, when I was asked to develop supplementary notes on WMD terrorism for inclusion in an intelligence assessment being prepared by a colleague on Osama bin Laden. The plan was for my work to be presented in a 'box', in the same way that newspaper and magazine articles hive off selected aspects of complex issues into side-panels. One thing led to another, and by the time the highly classified document was finalised and distributed, my detailed work on the risk of WMD terrorism had become the focus and bin Laden specifically had been relegated to the box. The events of September 11, 2001 were still a long way off.

Primed by this experience, I continued to follow the WMD issue and was well placed to attend an allied intelligence conference on WMD in the UK in 1999. Over a week a few dozen intelligence officers pored over the latest information and kicked around our ideas on every aspect of WMD, chemical and biological weapons in particular. The allied representatives naturally took the lead on the Middle East and Eastern Europe, including Iran, Iraq, Libya, Russia and Syria. The Australian team focussed on Asia, including China, India, Indonesia, North Korea, Pakistan and Vietnam.

At the 2001 conference there was a real feeling of accom-plishment among the hosting intelligence agencies for their key role in discovering Iraq's efforts to purchase the highly specified bulk aluminium tubing. Uncovering the convoluted China–Australia–Jordan–Iraq supply chain had been a real coup. Not only was involvement in the developing Iraq drama a rare occur-rence for the agencies, due to their Asia-Pacific focus, but their contribution had provided what was to be the second and final piece of evidence in the case that Iraq was trying to reconstitute its nuclear programme.

All the back-slapping was short-lived. Considerable uncer-tainty about the purpose of the tubes arose almost as soon as Iraq's efforts to obtain them were uncovered. In fact, experts from the International Atomic Energy Agency (IAEA) had seri-ous doubts about the claims right from the start – as far back as mid-2001 they were prepared only to acknowledge the dual-use potential of the material, and by the eve of the war they had ruled out the gas centrifuge possibility altogether. Notably the Director-General of the IAEA, Mohamed El Baradei, gave an effective public endorsement, well before the war, to the Iraqi claim that the tubes were intended only for the manufacture of short-range rockets. On 9 January 2003 he addressed the UN Security Council:

> The IAEA's analysis to date indicates that the specifications of the aluminum tubes sought by Iraq in 2001 and 2002 appear to be consistent with reverse engineering of rockets. While it would be possible to modify such tubes for the man-ufacture of centrifuges, they are not directly suitable for it.[7]

He was even more unequivocal on 7 March 2003:

92

Extensive field investigation and document analysis have failed to uncover any evidence that Iraq intended to use these 81 mm tubes for any project other than the reverse engineering of rockets ... the IAEA team has concluded that Iraq's efforts to import these aluminium tubes were not likely to have been related to the manufacture of centrifuges, and moreover that it was highly unlikely that Iraq could have achieved the considerable re-design needed to use them in a revived centrifuge programme.[8]

These comments only noted the technical unsuitability of the tubes. They didn't even begin to address the equally important matter of the unmistakable intelligence signature that would have been generated by any Iraqi gas centrifuge facility – by virtue of the large number of personnel involved in such a venture, the considerable quantities of uranium and electricity consumed, and the industrial complex required.

The IAEA's concern about the veracity of the aluminium tubes story was shared by US experts, so much so that the key pre-war US intelligence document, the October 2002 National Intelligence Estimate, referred to:

... the judgment of technical experts at the US Department of Energy (DOE) who have concluded that the tubes Iraq seeks to acquire are poorly suited for use in gas centrifuges to be used for uranium enrichment.[9]

Against this backdrop it was unsurprising that many intelligence officials in the US, the UK and Australia quickly started to back away from their initial assessment that the tubing was destined for use in an Iraqi nuclear programme. The US State

Department's Bureau of Intelligence and Research (INR), unlike the CIA, felt so strongly about it that it insisted on the following qualification being included in the National Intelligence Estimate:

> Iraq's efforts to acquire aluminium tubes is central to the argument that Baghdad is reconstituting its nuclear weapons programme, but INR is not persuaded that the tubes in question are intended for use as centrifuge rotors.[10]

The Chairman of the UK's Joint Intelligence Committee, John Scarlett, was just as concerned, and he was careful to caution Tony Blair's spin doctor, Alastair Campbell, to tone down the information in the UK's September 2002 dossier. Hence the inclusion of the following careful qualification at the end of the relevant section:

> Iraq has also made repeated attempts covertly to acquire a very large quantity (60,000 or more) of specialized aluminium tubes ... although there is no definitive intelligence that it is destined for a nuclear programme.[11]

Even in Australia the trust usually placed in the CIA was abandoned when it came to the aluminium tubes story. Commonsense and the views of the well-regarded INR took primacy, so much so that the highly classified assessments going to the government from ONA were full of equivocal judgements suggesting only that the tubes 'could' be intended for use in gas centrifuges – a clear reflection of the uncertainty about the issue throughout the broader Australian intelligence community.

None of the reservations about the accuracy of the Iraq

aluminium tubes story seemed to bother those determined to invade Iraq. They just ploughed on, kicking into high gear with a disinformation campaign that began with a *New York Times* front-page article on 8 September 2002. This was not the first time, and far from the last, that the US media fell over itself to act as a mouthpiece for the Bush administration:

> Over the last 14 months, Iraq has tried to buy thousands of specially designed aluminum tubes, which American officials believed were intended as components of centrifuges to enrich uranium. American officials said several efforts to arrange the shipment of the high-strength tubes were blocked or intercepted, but declined to say, citing the extreme sensitivity of the intelligence, where they came from or how they were stopped.[12]

From that point on there was no turning back – no admission whatsoever that the tubes story was already well and truly discredited, no hint that it was all a preposterous lie designed to win support for the invasion. Dick Cheney and National Security Advisor Condoleeza Rice immediately hit the talk shows. John Howard endorsed the evidence during a radio interview on 12 September 2002. Also on 12 September, George W. Bush told the UN General Assembly that, 'Iraq has made several attempts to buy high-strength aluminium tubes used to enrich uranium for a nuclear weapon.'[13] Alexander Downer told the Australian Parliament on 17 September that, 'There is evidence of a pattern of acquisition of equipment which could be used in a uranium enrichment programme.'[14] And Tony Blair told his parliament on 24 September that Saddam Hussein 'has attempted, covertly, to acquire 60,000 or more specialised aluminium tubes'.[15]

These lies about Iraq acquiring bulk aluminium tubing for use in a uranium-enriching gas centrifuge were echoed by the lies about Iraq having tried to purchase uranium in Niger. Each deception was of course alarming in its own right. Together they were outrageous, because together they meant that the entire case that Saddam was trying to reconstitute his nuclear programme was bogus. And if the nuclear story was removed from the official case for war – images of mushroom clouds and all – what remained was a much less compelling case.

How the Niger story ever got into the case for war beggars belief. The bundle of very badly forged documents that made up the 'intelligence' on the matter was so dubious as to make any claims to the contrary quite preposterous. Moreover, the US Embassy in the capital Niamey had by early 2002 already investigated the story and Ambassador Owens-Kirkpatrick had despatched cables to Washington debunking the issue.

And there was the Joe Wilson saga. Wilson was a former career diplomat who had been despatched to Niger in February 2002 – 'the CIA paid my expenses'[16] – to investigate the matter further. He quickly concluded there was simply no basis for the story that Iraq was attempting to purchase uranium from Niger: the structure of the business interests involved and the IAEA monitoring of both Iraq and Niger combined in such a way as to make any sale well-nigh impossible.

Wilson's findings were widely distributed, both throughout the US government and to close allies the UK and Australia. Wilson said publicly:

Before I left Niger, I briefed the ambassador on my findings, which were consistent with her own. I also shared my conclusions with members of her staff. In early March, I arrived in Washington and promptly provided a detailed briefing to the CIA. I later shared my conclusions with the State Department African Affairs Bureau.[17]

We know also that the information had reached INR and had been shared with allies some time in 2002, because as much has been said publicly by former senior INR officer Greg Thielmann, who retired from the Bureau in August 2002. I remember very well that ONA in Australia was aware in 2002 that the Niger story was fraudulent, and that on that basis alone half of the nuclear case against Iraq had collapsed. It is entirely unsurprising that ONA in particular should and would have known this key information in 2002, given its very close working relationship with the US agencies. During this time, too, it was the ONA Washington Liaison Officer's practice to call regularly on the State Department and relevant intelligence agencies, and to communicate diligently all relevant information back to Canberra over one of the secure voice, email or cable channels at their disposal.

In spite of this, almost every significant pro-war official speech in the US, the UK and Australia in the lead-up to the 2003 Iraq war ran the line that Iraq had tried to purchase uranium from Africa. The only exception to this was Powell's 5 February 2003 address to the UN Security Council – at least he had the good sense to leave the matter alone.

In the UK the claim was made repeatedly that the British intelligence services possessed additional information proving that Iraq had in fact attempted to procure uranium in Africa. However, that intelligence, so it was claimed, was collected by another country and was so sensitive that it couldn't be shared, even with the US. What rot. Sensitive intelligence is constantly being shared between the US, the UK and Australia – not to mention Canada and NZ – in contravention of the release conditions imposed by others.

Equally preposterous is the way in which the Australian government has stuck with its line that the Prime Minister, Defence Minister and Foreign Minister were all unaware that the Niger story was fraudulent when the Prime Minister used the claim during his 4 February 2003 address to the parliament. This apparent 'unawareness' is clearly inconsistent with official statements from ONA, the Department of Defence and the Department of Foreign Affairs, all of which have acknowledged that they knew in January 2003 that the Niger story was simply wrong. No satisfactory official explanation has ever been provided for this alarming disconnection, other than the claim that the three key government organisations were all in possession of the critical national security information, but that all three failed to pass it on to the Prime Minister and relevant ministers.

Accompanying the deceit concerning Iraq's nuclear ambitions was the absurd claim by Washington, London and Canberra that the war was legal – 'absurd' because the war could only have been legal if it was an act of self-defence in accordance with the UN Charter, or if Saddam had breached a UN Security Council resolution authorising war in the event of such a breach. Neither was the case.

First, the war was not consistent with the pre-condition for self-defence detailed in Article 51 of the Charter:

Nothing in the present Charter shall impair the inherent right of individual or collective self-defence if an armed attack occurs against a Member of the United Nations, until the Security Council has taken measures necessary to maintain international peace and security.[18]

In essence, self-defence is legal only when it occurs in response to an 'armed attack.' But Iraq had not attacked any regional country in the years prior to the 2003 invasion, let alone the US, the UK or Australia. Nor was it likely to attempt to do so in the foreseeable future, given its weak conventional military forces and its limited WMD programme.

Some proponents of the war went so far as to claim some sort of justification by extending the doctrine of self-defence to include *pre-emptive* self-defence; not unlike the justification Germany used in 1914 when it invaded Belgium to pre-empt an attack by France, and again in 1939 when it invaded Poland to pre-empt an attack by that country. It is precisely because of the dangerous nature of such a hybrid doctrine that the UN Charter does not include it as a legitimate justification for the use of force.

Pre-emptive use of force would in any case need to satisfy certain clear prerequisites to have any chance of being acceptable as a justification. The perceived threat must be imminent, and the response must be proportional, to name only two of these. Neither one of these commonsense criteria was satisfied by the official case for the Iraq war. Instead the US acted in conformity with the Bush administration's security doctrine, enshrined in *The National Security Strategy of the United States of America*:

For centuries, international law recognized that nations need not suffer an attack before they can lawfully take action to defend themselves against forces that present an imminent danger of attack. Legal scholars and international jurists often conditioned the legitimacy of preemption on the existence of an imminent threat – most often a visible mobilization of armies, navies, and air forces preparing to attack.

We must adapt the concept of imminent threat to the capabilities and objectives of today's adversaries. Rogue states and terrorists do not seek to attack us using conventional means. They know such attacks would fail. Instead, they rely on acts of terror and, potentially, the use of weapons of mass destruction – weapons that can be easily concealed, delivered covertly, and used without warning.

The United States has long maintained the option of preemptive actions to counter a sufficient threat to our national security. The greater the threat, the greater is the risk of inaction – and the more compelling the case for taking anticipatory action to defend ourselves, even if uncertainty remains as to the time and place of the enemy's attack. To forestall or prevent such hostile acts by our adversaries, the United States will, if necessary, act preemptively.[19]

So there it is – the US had made no secret of its preparedness to use force whenever and wherever it chose, especially if it could claim the pretext of a rogue state, WMD or terrorism. It is no wonder that the Iranians and North Koreans are so paranoid and so intent on acquiring their own nuclear deterrents (if Pyongyang is not merely scheming to obtain leverage with the international community).

Nor was the 2003 Iraq war legal on the basis of a breach of a UN Security Council Resolution whereby war was authorised specifically in the event of such a breach. Even so, the pro-war lobby contrived arguments along the following lines:

> ... the failure by Iraq to give up its weapons of mass destruction immediately is a material breach of resolution 1441 September 2002. The material breach of Res. 1441, terminates the ceasefire in Res. 687 ... An end to the ceasefire 'reactivates' resolution 678 of November 1990 authorising the use of 'all necessary means to uphold and implement Res. 660 (1990) and all subsequent relevant resolutions and to restore international peace and security.'[20]

This is mere legal mumbo-jumbo. Resolution 1441 did not in any way authorise the use of force or regime change in the event of any so-called 'material breach'. This is not only clear from the resolution itself, it was explicitly confirmed at the time by a number of UN Security Council members, as well as by the frantic attempts of the US and the UK, just before the war began, to force the passing of another resolution by the UN Security Council which specifically did authorise the use of force.

Saddam is a horrid man who flouted Security Council resolutions, and there is little doubt that one day Iraq will be a better place for his passing. And yes, the eventual humanitarian benefits of the war could, in a roundabout way, give the whole sorry episode some sort of partial legitimacy. But rarely was either regime change or the humanitarian benefit singled out before the war to justify the invasion. And neither of these was authorised as a justification for the war by a specific UN Security Council resolution, in what would have been the critical precondition for any such intervention to be regarded as legal under international law.

Saddam kept his adversaries guessing, in the face of persistent international demands for disarmament. Perhaps this was wise,

AXIS OF DECEIT

given that Iraq faced adversaries (usually of its own making) in
every corner. Think about that. Disarmament was demanded
although Iraq was squared off against Iran, Kuwait, Saudi Arabia,
Jordan, Israel, Syria and Turkey – all adversaries; many backed by
the US, many with sizeable arsenals of WMD. Even the Persian
Gulf was brimming with enemy warships.

Maybe Saddam Hussein was just a stupid man who completely misjudged the situation. Maybe he was misled by his
fawning minions. Maybe he thought a war was so clearly unjustified that no world leader would be crazy enough to start or
sign up to one. Maybe he thought the US would never risk a
war, or that the international community would intervene to
stop such madness. Maybe he thought he could win, either in the
short term or as part of some grand strategy involving a guerrilla
war and who knows what else. Maybe he knew he couldn't win
in a conventional sense, but that he could still score a moral victory by rolling over to reveal himself to be much less the villain
than his protagonists had been claiming. Maybe he'll still get the
last laugh.

BLAME GAME

The eyes are not responsible when the mind does the seeing.
—Publilius Syrus

The scale of the pre-war public scepticism about the official case for conflict was demonstrated by the extraordinary February 2003 demonstrations. The millions who hit the streets hardly needed access to intelligence advice to convince them that a war at that time was neither the most sensible nor the most ethical way to resolve the question of Iraq. For them – like me still on the inside – it was easy to come to the conclusion that Iraq did not pose a serious enough threat to justify a war, that there was too great a risk of things going terribly wrong, and that time still remained to explore other solutions. The protesters never bought the official line that Iraq possessed a massive arsenal of WMD, nor that it was co-operating actively with the broad Islamic extremist network linked to al Qaida.

The millions of pre-war sceptics were just the start of it. By May 2003 – less than a couple of months after the invasion – the number of concerned people was starting to swell as the

103

discrepancy grew between the official case for war and what was quickly becoming evident on the ground in Iraq. To the bitter disappointment of the advocates of the misadventure, the tide was turning. No WMD were being found. No evidence of active pre-war co-operation with al Qaida was being unearthed. The invading troops were increasingly being treated as occupiers rather than liberators. And the only realistic prospect now seemed to be a drawn-out slogging match against and beside a complex combination of jihadists and guerrilla and civil-war fighters. Bush, Blair and Howard must have thought in their quiet moments: it was not supposed to be anything like this. The precious dividends of their war were slipping through their fingers.

For a while, though, Washington, London and Canberra held the line. This was easy enough at first, given the understandable media focus on the success of the initial battle for Iraq. But by early May too many embarrassing questions were being asked too frequently, prompting Colin Powell to say desperately on 4 May, 'I'm absolutely sure that there are weapons of mass destruction there and the evidence will be forthcoming. We're just getting it just now.'[1] On the same day Donald Rumsfeld also stalled, offering the disingenuous observation that, 'We never believed that we'd just tumble over weapons of mass destruction in that country.'[2] Weeks later, on 26 May, the Chairman of the US Joint Chiefs of Staff, General Richard Myers, was still in denial – 'Given time, given the number of prisoners now that we're interrogating, I'm confident that we're going to find weapons of mass destruction.'[3]

Stalling in this way was rapidly coming to appear both evasive and deceitful, especially in light of the comments coming from the field. On 30 May 2003, for instance, the Commander of the 1st Marine Expeditionary Force, Lieutenant General James Conway, conceded to reporters:

It was a surprise to me ... that we have not uncovered weapons ... believe me, it's not for lack of trying. We've been to virtually every ammunition supply point between the Kuwaiti border and Baghdad, but they're simply not there.[4]

No wonder the troops in the field were getting restless. After all, by the time of Conway's concession the invading forces had swept through vast tracts of Iraq and teams of specialists had examined countless suspect sites. That Iraq's arsenal of alleged WMD would by now have been found had never been in doubt in any of the soldiers' minds. They, like everyone else, had heard Rumsfeld proclaim on 30 March that, 'We know where they are. They're in the area around Tikrit and Baghdad and east, west, south and north somewhat.'[5]

More of the same approach seemed unlikely to unearth an Iraqi arsenal of WMD or head off the growing public concern. The mood had changed. I for one responded to public interest in the matter by writing in the *Sydney Morning Herald* at the end of May 2003 that:

US intelligence on Iraq was badly skewed by political pressure, worst-case analysis and a stream of garbage-grade intelligence concocted by Iraqis desperate for US intervention in Iraq ...The CIA had clearly lost the plot if its October 2002 report on Iraq's weapons of mass destruction program was anything to go by ... US impatience to go for Iraq had very little to do with WMDs and an awful lot to do with US strategic and domestic interests.[6]

If the public mood was now sceptical, it met with no corresponding inclination in Washington, London or Canberra to admit fault or even error. During those first couple of months there was no shortage of false starts, many of which now serve to illustrate how the US, the UK and Australia sought to play the blame game over the unravelling case for war. Perhaps the most dramatic example remains the discovery of two trailers near Mosul, one by Kurdish forces in late April, the other by US forces in early May. To a layperson's eyes these appeared quite similar to the mobile WMD production facilities described by Powell during his 5 February 2003 UN speech. They were seized upon immediately by officials and a compliant media as unambiguous proof of Iraqi mischief. They were even given the status of actual weapons by George W. Bush on 29 May 2003 during an interview with Polish television:

> We found the weapons of mass destruction. We found biological laboratories. You remember when Colin Powell stood up in front of the word, and he said, Iraq has got laboratories, mobile labs to build biological weapons. They're illegal. They're against the United Nations resolutions, and we've so far discovered two. And we'll find more weapons as time goes by. But for those who say we haven't found the banned manufacturing devices or banned weapons, they're wrong, we found them.[7]

This was an extraordinary claim. For a start there was the deliberate dishonesty of Bush, to be talking like this when in Iraq the experts who had examined the trailers had already distanced themselves from the presumptive claim that the machinery was part of an Iraqi WMD programme. They had found no trace of any banned biological agent on the equipment and concluded that in any case the trailers would not be complete manufacturing plants. Their assessment, contained in a CIA–DIA joint report dated 28 May, included the following:

> ... units that we have not yet found would be needed to prepare and sterilize the media and to concentrate and possibly dry the agent, before the agent is ready for introduction into a delivery system, such as bulk-filled munitions.[8]

At the same time Bush was describing the trailers as 'weapons', his own experts had already advised that the Iraqi claim that the trailers were for manufacturing gas to fill balloons was a plausible one – 'Hydrogen production would be a plausible cover story for the mobile production units,' they wrote on the day before Bush's session with Polish television.

Just as disturbing was the way in which the compliant press latched onto the disinformation being fed to it by official contacts and briefing officers. Journalists, especially those who had signed up to the Iraq WMD story long before and whose professional reputations depended on a smoking gun being found, were desperate to push the line that the trailers were just what Powell had warned us about in the UN only a few months previously. Judith Miller from the *New York Times* led the pack, writing repeatedly about the significance of the trailers. Perhaps this would be acceptable if the press – and the officials too, I should add – were diligent in providing the relevant corrections and retractions. But they rarely were. Certainly, in regard to the Iraq war, many reporters and officials never paid anything close to the same degree of attention to the news that the trailers were not related to any WMD programme as they had to their own early reports on the matter. The result is that many people apparently still believe that the trailers were WMD-related. Or at least they did until April 2004, when Powell finally conceded the blind-ingly obvious, saying of the intelligence concerning the trailers, 'it appears not to be the case that it was that solid.'[9] Nor was this an isolated incident. On many occasions the media played up an inaccurate story, whether unintentionally or not, only to fail to report proportionally the accurate version of events.

Such ineptitude and willingness to perpetuate official disin-formation help to explain the enduring public misunderstanding of the Iraq war, especially in the US. But of course the failure of the press did not start with its poor performance during the war – it started so much earlier that many people were ill-equipped to understand properly the conduct of the war itself. This is especially important if research by academics from the University of Western Australia, Potsdam University and Plattsburgh State University of New York is anything to go by. They found that the less suspicious people were of the motives underpinning the Iraq conflict, the less able they were to discount disinformation upon its retraction. Summing up the findings in a letter to me, Professor Stephen Lewandowsky from the University of Western Australia wrote:

> In a nutshell, we show that people can discount misinfor-mation upon its retraction (i.e., if a previously stated 'fact' is later identified as erroneous) only if they are suspicious of the motives underlying the war. When suspicion is absent, people continue to believe in statements that they know to have been retracted. Perhaps not surprisingly, suspicion var-ied between countries, with Australians and Germans being fairly suspicious of the motives underlying the war. The American sample, by contrast, showed little suspicion – and hence was unable to discount misinformation. In addition,

about a third of the people in the American sample falsely remembered that WMD had been found in Iraq.[10]

It was a consolation prize of sorts for the architects of the conflict that anyone believed that the promised Iraqi arsenal of WMD had actually been found. Unfortunately it was a prize of diminishing value, as day by day more information emerged to discredit further the case for war. Perhaps the biggest single set-back was David Kay's departure in disgust from his post as the head of the Iraq Survey Group (ISG) in January 2004.

A long-time critic of Saddam and loyal supporter of Bush and his case for war, Kay had been appointed in mid-2003 to lead the hunt for WMD after months of fruitless searching by the occupation forces. He was a true believer, confident that Iraq's arsenal of WMD would soon be found once his people took over the reins from the Pentagon. But the reality was that he would have virtually no more success than those who had already been trying for months to find the mysterious arsenal. During a newspaper interview he described his slow realisation and his 'great unease' that so many of his assumptions about Iraq had been unfounded:

> It wasn't a eureka moment. It was a slow accretion from June on. I had millions of dollars of reward money that I could have paid for information on weapons and believe me, if someone had come in and said this is where they're hidden, we would have taken care of them for the rest of their life. The fact that no one came forward for it was a worrying concern.[11]

By the time Kay returned to the US in September 2003 to

deliver his interim report, he was sure that Iraq did not have a massive arsenal of WMD. However, he resisted delivering the bad news. What he did have to say, however, clearly forewarned officials and observers alike of what was to come:

> ... our understanding of the status of Iraq's WMD program was always bounded by large uncertainties and had to be heavily caveated.
>
> We have not yet found stocks of weapons ...
>
> Despite evidence of Saddam's continued ambition to acquire nuclear weapons, to date we have not uncovered evidence that Iraq undertook significant post-1998 steps to actually build nuclear weapons or produce fissile material.[12]

Kay was certainly not the only main player in the Iraq Survey Group starting to fear as much. In October 2003 Brigadier Stephen Meekin, the Australian in charge of the key ISG organisation, the Joint Captured Enemy Material Exploitation Centre, told reporters that pre-war claims that Iraq was importing components for a nuclear weapons programme were simply wrong. In one particular admission that must have sent the Australian government into a rage, he noted, 'By and large our judgement is that sanctions have been pretty good.'[13] The significance of such a statement cannot be overestimated, not just because of the seniority and credibility of the witness – I know Meekin and can vouch personally for both his professionalism and integrity – but also because of the gap it reveals between the views of the exasperated weapons searchers in Iraq and the simultaneous public assertions of Bush, Blair and Howard that the jury was still out on the question of whether or not Iraq possessed a massive arsenal of WMD.

Make no mistake about any of this. There had obviously been a worrying disconnection between reality and the official statements coming out of Washington, London and Canberra since well before the war began. In some peoples' minds that disconnection might, for a time, have been put down to an almost excusable stuff-up. By late 2003, however, there was no possibility that Bush, Blair and Howard were unaware of the true situation in Iraq or that they were in some form of understandable denial. No, they were well aware of the fix they were in, but decided to deal with it with more prevarications, fabrications, distortions and exaggerations. Lies beget lies, as they say. It came as no surprise when the US government resorted to vilifying Meekin. The press reported that, 'A US government official, unwilling to be identified by name or agency, said Brigadier Meekin was not qualified to make that judgement.'[14] I hope Meekin hadn't expected to have a more successful career.

Not long afterwards, the possibility of any further stonewalling by Bush, Blair and Howard came abruptly to an end with Kay's surprise resignation. Frustrated by the absence of anything resembling an Iraqi WMD arsenal, he told a US Senate hearing on 28 January 2004 that, 'We were all wrong ... and that is most disturbing.'[15] This was a dramatic development, not least for me personally, because with Kay's admission came finally the unambiguous official acknowledgement of the accuracy of a key aspect of my own assessment of Iraq's WMD programme – 'Iraq's weapons of mass destruction programme is, I believe, genuinely contained ... their programme now is disjointed and limited. It's not a national WMD programme like they used to have.'[16] These were my words in the *Bulletin* magazine on the day after my resignation from ONA, more than a week before the war began.

I should acknowledge in this regard that my own assessment had been that Iraq probably did possess some chemical and biological weapons, though not in quantities posing a serious enough threat to justify a war. The apparent absence of any weapons surprised me as much as it did many other people in the intelligence world. There had been too much evidence to the contrary to confidently draw the conclusion that there were no weapons whatsoever. I was less surprised, though, that no weapons had actually been used. To my mind this scenario had always been a 'could', rather than a 'would', in particular because of the questionable utility of any limited Iraqi use of WMD given the near certainty of a disproportionate US response. Significantly, it had been long understood in ONA that Washington would seriously consider using nuclear weapons against any country, including Iraq, that tried to use WMD against it. The death toll would have been horrendous. Tens of thousands more Iraqis would have died at the very least.

After the start of the war I was confident for a time that evidence of small quantities of Iraqi WMD would be found. But this confidence soon gave way to doubt that any weapons would be uncovered at all, probably because they had been secretly destroyed or were too well hidden. In fact, at a public meeting in Cooma on 21 March 2003 – only ten days after my resignation and one day after the start of the war – I spoke of the moral victory Saddam could still win if he had thought to destroy the evidence of his non-compliance with UN Security Council resolutions. Perhaps he did, although with the benefit of hindsight I tend now to agree with Kay's breathtaking eventual assessment that, 'There were no stockpiles of weapons of mass destruction at the time of the war.'[17]

Nevertheless, the proponents of the invasion of Iraq have never been ones to let either the experts or the facts get in the way of a good story. Donald Rumsfeld, for example, responded to Kay's assessment by telling the Senate Armed Services Committee in February 2004 that inspectors needed more time before they could reach final conclusions. The Defense Secretary offered a broad range of explanations for the Iraq Survey Group's failure to find the promised WMD arsenal, notably including the possibility that Iraq had actually transferred these weapons to one or more other countries. This is a canny line of argument, one that in a single unverifiable sweep asserts that the official case for war was honest and accurate, and that the politically profitable national security issue must be kept alive because of the continued existence of those regimes evil enough to have co-operated with Saddam.

Unfortunately for Rumsfeld and the others who parroted this line, there was no evidence to support it, especially in reference to Syria, the obvious candidate. Intelligence material – in particular sigint and imagery – certainly pointed to movement of items out of Iraq in the lead-up to the war, but this information was vague and did not in itself provide any basis for the claim that WMD-related material was being secreted out of Iraq to Syria, or to anywhere else for that matter. The only certainty was, and is, that much if not all of this activity was related to the significant smuggling industry servicing Iraq, which thrived during the period of UN sanctions. ONA intelligence assessments going to government before my resignation were careful to downplay the possibility of WMD-related material being smuggled out of Iraq. Instead they focussed on a much more likely scenario: members of Saddam's and other senior Baath Party members' families, along with their belongings, were being moved out of Iraq in the months leading up to the conflict.

The efforts of Rumsfeld and others to downplay Kay's concerns about the official case for war were to amount to nothing. In the end Kay's Senate testimony was more effective than spin, and his response to Senator John McCain's line of questioning too powerful:

McCAIN: Do you believe that we need an independent, outside investigation?
KAY: Senator –
McCAIN: You don't have to answer that if you don't choose to, Dr. Kay. It's not a fair question.
KAY: It's really what goes to the heart of the integrity of our own process. I generally believe that it's important to acknowledge failure. I also think we've got enough history to understand that closed orders and secret societies, whether they be religious or governmental, are the groups that have the hardest time reforming themselves in the face of failure without outside input.

I must say, my personal view, and it's purely personal, is that in this case you will finally determine that it is going to take an outside inquiry, both to do it and to give yourself and the American people the confidence that you have done it.[18]

'Personal view' or not, Kay's concerns about the case for war and his call for an investigation effectively forced the issue in Washington, London and Canberra. Within days all three governments announced the establishment of new inquiries into the war, all intended apparently to go to the heart of how we had invaded a country for reasons now discredited. I say 'new', because by early 2004 there had already been all sorts of apparent investigations into the war in addition to the hearings in Washington. And I say 'apparently' and 'apparent' because there is no evidence to suggest that any of the inquiries have been, or will be, anything other than political stunts designed to shift blame from the members of the governments who decided to invade Iraq.

First off the block was the investigation by the British Foreign Affairs Committee in mid-2003, which sought to:

> ... establish whether the Foreign and Commonwealth Office, within the Government as a whole, presented accurate and complete information to Parliament in the period leading up to military action in Iraq, particularly in respect of weapons of mass destruction.[19]

A commendable mission, I should say. Unfortunately it turned out to be just a pro-war forum incapable of independent and honest thought. In return for the millions of pounds it must have cost the British tax-payer, the government-dominated committee – with supporting performances from a handful of eager Tories – returned worthless findings such as:

> We conclude that it is too soon to tell whether the Government's assertions on Iraq's chemical and biological weapons will be borne out.
>
> We conclude that the accuracy of most of the claims in relation to Iraq's nuclear weapons programme can only be judged once the Survey Group has gained access to the relevant scientists and documentation.

> We conclude that without access to the intelligence or to those who handled it, we cannot know if it was in any respect faulty or misinterpreted.[20]

Then there was the inquiry by Lord Hutton, again in the UK, established to inquire into the circumstances surrounding the death of the leading DIS expert on WMD, Dr David Kelly. Although this was more a coronial inquest than an inquiry into the Iraq war, high hopes were held that Hutton would exercise his freedom of inquiry to shed some light on the broader matter of the UK's involvement in the war. After all, Kelly had apparently committed suicide following a tormenting period in the public spotlight after being named by the British government as the source of the BBC story that the government had 'sexed up' the case for war.

Again we were let down, Hutton opting to focus only on the circumstances surrounding Kelly's death and quite specific matters relating to the UK's September 2002 dossier, *Iraq's Weapons of Mass Destruction: The Assessment of the British Government*. In my view Hutton was clearly too unfamiliar with the world of intelligence to have been capable of assessing accurately the British government's behaviour over Iraq. Hence, for example, his bland treatment of the evidence about the politicisation of the British intelligence community, which really should have been treated as political dynamite. For instance:

> Intelligence staff ... did not argue that the intelligence relating to the 45 minutes claim should not have been included in the dossier but they did suggest that the wording in which the claim was stated in the dossier was too strong and that instead of the dossier stating 'we judge' that 'Iraq has: –

military plans for the use of chemical and biological weapons, including against its own Shia population. Some of these weapons are deployable within 45 minutes of an order to use them', the wording should state 'intelligence suggests'.

However I consider that the possibility cannot be completely ruled out that the desire of the Prime Minister to have a dossier which, whilst consistent with the available intelligence, was as strong as possible in relation to the threat posed by Saddam Hussein's WMD, may have subconsciously influenced Mr Scarlett and the other members of the JIC to make the wording of the dossier somewhat stronger than it would have been if it had been contained in a normal JIC assessment.[21]

Another missed opportunity.

Meanwhile the Australian government was doing everything possible to avoid any inquiry into any aspect of Australia's involvement in the Iraq war. However, not even the Prime Minister's legendary unaccountability could deflect the accumulating pressure in Australia for an inquiry. By mid-June the opposition-controlled Senate referred to the Parliamentary Joint Committee on ASIO, ASIS and DSD the need for an investigation of the raw intelligence and assessments relating to Iraq, as well as the government's public use of that material. It was less than a perfect solution given the inquiry's limited scope and power, but it was better than nothing, especially in the face of Howard's refusal to instigate a more thoroughgoing investigation.

There was no reason for confidence that the Australian inquiry would be any more searching than its British counterparts. The members of the Joint Committee were mostly from the government, and even those from the opposition came from their party's pro-war faction. Before the committee had even started to take evidence, the head of the inquiry, David Jull, had indicated to the media that he expected his findings to back up the government's case for war. Moreover the draft report was circulated to stakeholders for vetting prior to release, purportedly to ensure there would be no accidental disclosure of classified material. The broader purpose of this vetting was exposed by the head of ONA when he conceded in a separate Senate hearing in mid–February 2004 that his agency had in fact 'looked at some of the judgements in the draft report'.[22] Well, what an interesting way to run a country – agencies being investigated for malpractice are empowered to review the findings against them as long as it suits the government's political aims. Curiously, too, the committee's report shows that the senior ONA strategic analyst responsible for Iraq did not appear as a witness – in other words the star witness didn't give evidence. Clearly someone didn't want the Joint Committee to unearth the whole story, and I'm sure it wasn't the analyst himself.

In the end much of the report released on 1 March 2004 was unsurprising, focussing on the self-evident though limited failure of the intelligence agencies to assess accurately the threat posed by Iraq. As far as they went, the inquiry's recommendations were sound. The final recommendation was inevitable in light of the concurrent controversy and the seemingly daily revelations in the US and the UK:

> The Committee recommends there should be an independent assessment of the performance of the intelligence agencies, conducted by an experienced former intelligence expert with full access to all the material, which will report

to the National Security Committee of Cabinet and which, in light of the matters raised by the consideration of the pre-war intelligence on Iraq, will recommend any changes that need to take place for the better functioning of the agencies.[23]

Much more surprising was the criticism in the Australian Joint Committee's report of the behaviour of the Australian government in regard to the Iraq war. Consider the following:

Therefore, the case made by the government was that Iraq possessed WMD in large quantities and posed a grave and unacceptable threat to the region and the world, particularly as there was a danger that Iraq's WMD might be passed to terrorist organisations.

This is not the picture that emerges from an examination of all the assessments provided to the Committee by Australia's two analytical agencies.[24]

Serious stuff, going well beyond the tripe that had come out of the UK. Even more dramatic were the observations offered subsequently to the Australian Parliament by a senior member of the Committee, Kim Beazley:

What this report makes amply clear is that there were deficiencies in intelligence and in our intelligence structures. There was never, however ... emphatically delivered hard advice without some form of qualification attached. The exaggeration and the sense of immediacy was the work of politicians, outside the intelligence advice they were being presented with – at least from the Australian agencies and,

I would suggest, their American and British counter-parts. Insofar as that internal intelligence reporting came close on rare occasions to government presentation, it can be seen, at least in part, as a response to unusual pressures placed on them by the atmosphere created by the political leadership – not pressure by the political leadership – which was determined on a course to war.[25]

Although this represents a degree of progress, I have little confidence in the next round of American, British and Australian inquiries into the Iraq war. Maybe I'll be pleasantly surprised, but I doubt it, if only because all three inquiries are focussed on the intelligence underpinning the case for war rather than on the crucial question of whether or not the respective governments misused that information in any way. This is not to say that the performances of the spies and the bureaucrats who manage them are not important. Clearly they are, so much so that I've devoted separate chapters to them in this book. But they are only a part of the explanation of how we got ourselves into such a mess in Iraq in the first place. Any serious autopsy needs to address all of the issues if it is to be a useful undertaking.

Bush's inquiry takes the cake for its shameless effort to shift American attention off Washington's case for war until well after the next presidential election. The cynicism is breathtaking – Bush personally selected the members of the 'independent' panel, Bush personally determined its terms of reference, and Bush has directed it to report by 31 March 2005, well after the November 2004 presidential election.

Predictably, not far behind Bush is Howard. The Australian leader is more cunning. He judged, quite rightly, that the sceptical Australian electorate would not accept a report date likely to fall after the next election (possible at any time before early 2005). Instead he has adopted the opposite approach, hand-picking a former senior intelligence official for the job, but not providing him with the time, the legal authority or the freedom of inquiry to achieve anything more than a quick rehash of the previous Australian inquiry.

As is often the case, the UK inquiry looks better at first glance. Given the British track record, however, we'll have to wait and see if it amounts to another Blair whitewash. Not that we'll have to wait long – as in Australia, the inquiry has been given very little time to do its work, which consists of little more than a quick review of the intelligence underpinning the official UK case for war. Ominously, the latest British inquiry, like the new US and Australian ventures, will not focus on the political judgements underpinning the war. 'The issue of good faith was determined by the Hutton inquiry,'[26] Blair is already on record as saying.

In playing the blame game over Iraq, a key tactic of Bush, Blair and Howard has been to re-engineer the official justification for the war. The invasion of Iraq was sold to us on the basis of that country possessing a massive arsenal of WMD and co-operating actively with terrorists. As that explanation quickly and inevitably fell apart, the three leaders were left to contort like unbalanced gymnasts desperately trying to stay on a beam.

In regard to WMD, the story changed from knowing that Iraq had an arsenal of WMD to knowing that it was involved in weapons-related programmes. Tony Blair's rhetoric is typical, although countless American and Australian examples could be provided. On 18 March 2003, Blair scoffed at any suggestion that Saddam had no WMD, saying:

We are now seriously asked to accept that in the last few years, contrary to all history, contrary to all intelligence, he decided unilaterally to destroy the weapons. Such a claim is palpably absurd.[27]

By 8 July of the same year, Blair claimed instead, 'I have absolutely no doubt at all that we will find evidence of weapons of mass destruction programmes, no doubt at all.'[28]

More recently the emphasis has shifted yet again, this time to Iraq's 'intent'. In other words, we know Iraq *wanted* WMD, regardless of what we might or might not find in the way of actual weapons themselves. Brilliant – almost disprovable. Colin Powell took it for a test-drive on 2 February 2004, telling the *Washington Post*:

With respect to intent, Saddam Hussein and his regime clearly had the intent. They never lost it. It's an intent that manifested itself many years ago when they actually used such horrible weapons against their enemies in Iran, and against their own people. It's a fact.[29]

The 'intent' line will clearly be the focus of Kay's successor, Charles Duelfer, who told a Senate committee that, 'The new area of focus I have initiated for ISG is that of regime intent.'[30]

What of the other pillar of the official case for war, the Iraqi links to al Qaida? For a long time the advocates of the war were spared much public scrutiny of this claim, thanks to the understandable focus on Iraq's alleged WMD. Perhaps, too, it was simply discounted out of hand by the very many people who understood the improbability of co-operation between Saddam's secular regime and the broad Islamic extremist network linked to al Qaida.

If Iraq was once completely unrelated to the 'War on Terror', however, this is no longer the case. Terrorism has become central to the Iraq issue, because the country has now become a magnet for jihadists in much the way that Soviet-occupied Afghanistan did during the 1980s. In other words, the Iraq war has managed to turn a country unrelated to the so-called 'War on Terror' into a central front in the campaign.

What turns this into a potential political disaster for Bush, Blair and Howard is the growing public realisation that the war has increased the terrorist threat more broadly. The invasion and occupation have fuelled hatred of the US and its close allies, especially given the absence of WMD and the prospect of a lengthy and harsh occupation. It is also now public knowledge that the possibility of fuelling the terrorist threat was well known in Washington, London and Canberra, as evidenced by the February 2003 UK Joint Intelligence Committee report that was shared with both the US and the Australian governments. In its Iraq inquiry, the British Intelligence and Security Committee described the relevant finding of the JIC report as follows:

> In their assessment *International Terrorism: War with Iraq*, dated 10 February 2003, the JIC ... judged that in the event of imminent regime collapse there would be a risk of transfer of such material, whether or not as a deliberate Iraqi regime policy. The JIC assessed that al Qaida's associated groups continued to represent by far the greatest threat to Western interests, and that threat would be heightened by military action against Iraq.[31]

The problem is compounded because the Iraq war has fundamentally diminished the capacity of all three countries to combat terrorism. Intelligence resources have been redirected from counter-terrorism to Iraq-related targets and issues. The significance of this cannot be underestimated, because intelligence capabilities are scarce – there is little 'excess' capacity – and any unnecessary tasking almost invariably results in a reduction of effort on other critical tasks. Although this is felt most immediately in the technical collection agencies, where capabilities can be redirected most easily and quickly, it also affects other agencies, in particular smaller outfits such as ONA where the establishment of the National Intelligence Watch Office, for any purpose, essentially drains the whole organisation of personnel.

Perhaps the most worrying way in which the Iraq war has seriously hindered the fight against terrorism, however, is how it has forced the premature withdrawal of military forces from Afghanistan. This country had always been central to the 'War on Terror'. In 2002, however, only months into the war there, and well before the Taliban and al Qaida had been defeated, the withdrawal of most foreign troops began as the US and the UK started to shift their focus to the invasion of Iraq. Only the Kabul-focussed International Stabilisation Force and a relatively tiny additional contingent were left to continue mobile offensive operations beyond the capital. In early 2004, the US had only around 15,000 troops committed to operations in Afghanistan compared with well over 100,000 in Iraq. Well, the Taliban and al Qaida are now resurgent in Afghanistan, while over 100,000 American, British and Australian troops are bogged down in Iraq. It's enough to encourage the more cynical among us to think either that some of our politicians actually want their

'War on Terror' to go on indefinitely, or that our so-called lead-ers are dangerously incompetent.

Maybe 'dangerously incompetent' is a larger part of the story than we care to consider, if we can put any store in the recent rev-elations from Washington. In *The Price of Loyalty*, Paul O'Neill describes how during Cabinet meetings the President was like a 'blind man in a room full of deaf people'.[32] In *Against All Enemies*, Richard Clarke recalls the blank look on the National Security Advisor's face when he first briefed America's top security offi-cial on al Qaida: 'As I briefed Rice on al Qaida, her facial expres-sion gave me the impression that she had never heard the term before.'[33]

John Howard's complete lack of interest in most off-shore matters was a frequent source of amusement and concern in ONA while I worked there. Time and time again important issues were not assessed because the judgement was made that Howard would not be interested. On many other occasions assessments were returned from his office unread – this being readily appar-ent because only those reports that his adviser knew his boss would be interested in reading were marked up with annotations and highlights and sent through to him. Howard seemed only interested in issues that were linked directly to his political self-interest and the term of his government. Longer-term matters in which Australia might have been more active, such as addressing the causes of global terrorism, were given scant attention.

Responding to the terrorist attacks in Spain in early 2004 was always going to be difficult for the British and Australian govern-ments. In one sickening day, all the talk that the Iraq war had made the world a safer place was revealed as nonsense. Given the parallels between Spain's strong support for Washington over Iraq and their own fervent cheerleading, it was unsurprising that

London and Canberra moved as quickly as they did to try to distance themselves politically from the Spanish tragedy. British Foreign Secretary Jack Straw, for instance, told the British media, 'I do not believe we are less safe as a result of the activity we have taken [in Iraq].'[34] His Australian counterpart, Alexander Downer, was just as adamant, saying, 'We're deeply unpopular with al Qaida because we fight al Qaida, because we're against al Qaida and because they are against our regime.'[35]

Many people, it appears, were not persuaded by these arguments. One Australian Newspoll found that 65 per cent of those polled believed that the Iraq war had increased the risk of terrorist attack. I suspect the assessment of many in that majority was based on little more than commonsense. Others were probably influenced by the expert opinions of people such as the Australian Federal Police Commissioner, Mick Keelty, who enraged the Australian government when he made this public comment on the Madrid attacks:

Well, I think we've said all along this is an uphill battle. This is a marathon, not a sprint. The reality is, if this turns out to be Islamic extremists responsible for this bombing in Spain, it's more likely to be linked to the position that Spain and other allies took on issues such as Iraq. And I don't think anyone's been hiding the fact that we do believe that ultimately one day, whether it be in one month's time, one year's time, or ten years' time, something will happen. And no-one can guarantee it won't. And I think there's a level of honesty that has to exist here in terms of what the problems are here, not only in Australia but in our region.[36]

Nor is Keelty the only official counter-terrorism expert to believe that the world is now a more dangerous place. His British colleague, London police chief Sir John Stevens, had this to say:

> It would be miraculous if, with all the terrorist resources arranged against us, terrorists did not get through, and given that some are prepared to give their own lives, it would be inconceivable that someone does not get through to London.[37]

Neither one of these experts sounded remotely like George W. Bush during his 2004 State of the Union Address, when he asserted that, 'For all who love freedom and peace, the world without Saddam Hussein's regime is a better and safer place.'[38]

In conclusion I note another curious aspect of the post-invasion management of the official case for war – the back-flip on 'regime change' by the leaders of the UK and Australia. Unlike George W. Bush, they were very careful to exclude the removal of Saddam from their official case for war, insisting instead that it was essentially his refusal to disarm that was the justification. Presumably Blair and Howard thought this divergence from the US's position would give them better cover legally. Blair told the British Parliament on 25 February 2003 that:

> I detest his [Saddam's] regime. But even now he can save it by complying with the UN's demand. Even now, we are prepared to go the extra step to achieve disarmament peacefully. I do not want war. I do not believe anyone in this House wants war. But disarmament peacefully can only happen with Saddam's active co-operation.[39]

Howard took a similar line, responding as follows to a journalist's pointed question on 13 March 2003 concerning the possibility of regime change:

> Well, I would have to accept that if Iraq had genuinely disarmed, I couldn't justify on its own a military invasion of Iraq to change the regime. I've never advocated that. Much in all as I despise the regime.[40]

Listening to Blair and Howard after the invasion, you'd be forgiven for thinking that all pre-war talk of this kind had never occurred. Now the talk is all about the liberation of the Iraqi people and the wonderful freedom they enjoy. Yet neither the US nor the UK exercised their right before the war to seek a specific UN Security Council resolution that would have authorised the use of force in Iraq on humanitarian grounds.

Meanwhile Bush and Blair have even been nominated for the Nobel Peace Prize.

Although the prospects for Iraq are unclear.

Although the war encouraged the proliferation of WMD by sending a signal to the US's adversaries that they need to develop nuclear weapons to deter US aggression.

Although the war increased the risk of terrorism by inflaming hatred of the US and its allies.

Although the war buffeted the United Nations.

And although the war has diminished the credibility of our leaders, and intelligence services, at a time when we sorely need to have confidence in both.

PUBLIC DISSERVICE

The deterioration of a government begins almost
always by the decay of its principles.
—Montesquieu

T
he 2003 Iraq war is a striking example of the perils of naivety. Many people never properly understood the intricacies of the issue or the machinations of their political leaders as they manoeuvred around it. Too many people, for instance, not understanding the crucial relevance of the unsuccessful US and UK pre-war efforts to secure a UN Security Council resolution specifically authorising war, were ill-equipped to assess the irrelevance of the post-war official claims that the superseded Resolution 1441 had legalised the use of force. In other words, with ignorance came political vulnerability. And with vulnerability came – as it so often seems to – the shysters keen to capitalise on the moment.

As the scale and the complexity of the deceit grew, it was more and more difficult to get at the truth. For some the issue became too big to comprehend. In the midst of lies that were never admitted and the terrible unfolding consequences of the invasion, it was easier to look away than to try to make sense of it all. No wonder that so many people withdrew into their familiar personal spaces.

Apathy to varying degrees was both a cause and a consequence of the naivety in our respective communities. Nowhere was this apathy more apparent than in Australia, where months sometimes passed with barely a ripple caused by either the deceitful official case for war or the terrible mess created by the misadventure. Some observers suggest that this can be explained by Australia's small contribution and lack of casualties. Maybe so, but I've long felt that the underlying explanation is much more complex and far more worrying – that the lackadaisical Australian approach to the war and its consequences has its origins more in racism and selfishness than in the mere absence of bodybags.

The underlying xenophobia in Australia is a curious thing in light of our successful multiculturalism. In 2004 I accepted an invitation to Friday prayers at Australia's largest mosque from the Mufti, Shaykh Taj Aldin al-Hilali. I had sensed that the Islamic community felt ostracised, in part because of the suspicion of 'foreigners' that the Australian government has fostered since September 11, and I was keen to show my support. Even so, I was not prepared for the restlessness I encountered among the members of the proud congregation. They knew they were on the defensive and were desperate for the social justice that is their right.

Good government would exercise leadership in order to ameliorate this dreadful situation, which fractures the Australian community in ways that will take generations to heal. Instead, the Howard government has moved in the opposite direction, driving wedges into the social fault-lines it judges likely to return a political advantage.

We expect governments to act responsibly and honestly; the slide in public sentiment from scepticism to cynicism reflects a feeling of betrayal. In particular the refusal to accept responsibility for the war on Iraq has gone well beyond any acceptable level, and there is no sign of any end to the evasion. It encompasses far more than the collective inability of Bush, Blair and Howard to concede that their well-worn case for war was wrong. Ultimately, leaders of nations are responsible for everything that happens by their hand. Those who decided to wage this war are responsible for the harm that it has done to the UN, just as they are responsible for every person who has died, or been injured, terrorised or in any other way affected by the conflict. And this is only the start of the long list of things for which the architects of this war must one day accept responsibility. Why? Because that's what leadership consists of – accepting personal responsibility for your decisions and those of your staff, rather than saying no-one is responsible or blaming someone else.

The terrible October 2002 Bali bombing provides another example of this lack of accountability, because the Australian government was forewarned of the possibility of such an attack but failed to do anything about it. Soon after the tragedy, one of the senior Indonesia analysts in ONA showed me the assessment he'd written alerting the government to the possibility. Although I was impressed by his analysis, I thought nothing of it until May 2002, when I recollected the assessment during a discussion about Bali with ABC television journalist Andrew Fowler. Fowler was obviously intrigued by the information and started to search for more on the topic. His interest was apparently detected by others, who proceeded to release early ONA's submission to the Senate inquiry into the bombing. It makes for very interesting reading:

> In a report of 27 September 2001, ONA assessed ... the threats by Muslim extremists of violence against the citizens and assets of the US and its close allies must be taken seriously ... no sign that Laskar Jihad plans to target tourist hotels on Lombok or Bali, though extremists see them as havens of Western decadence ... even so, a tourist hotel in Bali would be an important symbolic target, damaging Indonesia's standing and its debilitated economy ... ONA also felt it desirable to draw to the Government's attention by means other than written reports its conclusion on the existence of a regional extremist network with connections to al Qaida. It therefore asked to see the Foreign Minister, Mr Downer, to provide a briefing on this issue ... This briefing took place in two sections on 18 and 19 June 2002 ... in response to a question from Mr Downer about possible targets, Bali, Riau and Singapore were assessed to be attractive targets for Jemaah Islamiyah ... International hotels, nightclubs and airlines/airports were assessed as being high on terrorists' target lists.[1]

Downer was warned clearly and repeatedly about the risks to Australians in Bali, yet he took no action to ensure the travel advisory was upgraded. This in itself is obviously appalling, but it's not the end of the matter. Since that terrible night in Indonesia, he has repeatedly denied that he received any actionable warning from Australian intelligence agencies or that he is in any way responsible for a failure to alert travellers to Bali to the risk.

The idea that the end justifies the means has taken hold in the political process. We see this on a grand scale in the aftermath of the Iraq war, where the need to remove an evil dictator is now advanced as the standard justification for having invaded a sovereign state without international endorsement. A new big lie masks the underlying habitual dishonesty that brought us into the war in the first place. Tellingly, in one survey – requested by US Democrat Henry Waxman – 237 specific misleading statements were found in the 125 speeches, press conferences, briefings, interviews, written statements and testimonies made by George W. Bush, Dick Cheney, Donald Rumsfeld, Colin Powell and Condoleeza Rice before and during the war. Staggering but true, and all the worse considering that the survey carefully excluded all statements that appeared to be wrong only with the benefit of hindsight.

All too often in the lead-up to the Iraq war, governments manipulated the flow of information to their political opponents. I saw this form of control first-hand at least three times during my ONA service, twice when I was required to brief Labor Party leader Simon Crean on border security issues, and again when I was part of a larger team briefing Crean on a range of matters.

In essence, the briefings were allowed at the discretion of the Prime Minister's office. From this fact alone flow all sorts of benefits to those in power, notably including the opportunity to gain some control over the Opposition's line of political attack simply by turning the flow of information on and off. The act of providing briefings brings the Opposition into the government's confidence; it encourages some degree of bipartisanship and helps to diminish the possibility of public spats over national security issues that might weaken the government's position. Moreover the Opposition comes to relish the briefings – so much so that it learns not to use any of the material in its attacks against the government, lest it lose its access to the precious information.

Very rarely this arrangement breaks down, as it did when Crean's successor, Mark Latham, enraged the government by telling the parliament that intelligence briefings had convinced him that the government's Iraq policy was a 'fiasco'.[2] Howard appeared to suffer an apoplexy. He accused Latham of dishonesty, and to back up this accusation the Defence Minister, Robert Hill, announced that at future briefings the Opposition leader would be accompanied by a witness to ensure that he could not lie about what had been said to him. This was bad news for Latham – he clearly won't be invited to many more intelligence briefings while leader of the Opposition – but it was worse news for ordinary citizens, because the government's pre-occupation with political self-interest ultimately degrades the public debate about national security and diminishes the country's capacity and willingness to respond to real threats.

Not too much should be made of Hill's witness requirement. The attendance of government staffers in briefings to the Opposition has long been commonplace; it helps to ensure that officials do not drift or are not drawn into criticism of the government. While government policy is not meant to be discussed directly, the government makes a serious effort to ensure that intelligence briefings for Opposition leaders are always consistent with the current position. In other words, only material that supports the government's position is allowed to be conveyed. The dishonesty inherent in this strictly enforced government control has unfortunate consequences. During my third session with Crean, the ONA officers briefing him on Iraq presented an unbalanced assessment of the situation in Iraq in general and the state of Saddam's WMD programme in particular. Everyone from ONA knew that they were party to something much less than a frank and fearless briefing. No wonder, then, that Crean's team had a difficult time coming to grips with the shortfalls and lies in the official case for war. Perhaps this helps to explain, too, why the Greens and the Democrats made more accurate criticisms of the official case for war – they'd been fed less disinformation by the government.

The Crean briefing was telling in another way, too: what was said was not as important as what was not said. Intelligence material can have an almost intoxicating effect on the uninitiated, who can all too easily be won over by the grave nature and mysterious origins of what they are allowed to see. When material is excluded that might warn them to be wary about a particular aspect of the matter in question, they are rarely in a position to know any better. In effect, a tightly controlled supply of intelligence material to selected politicians can easily incline them towards a particular line of reasoning, and away from other, equally important areas.

In the aftermath of the Iraq war, much has been revealed about the politicisation of the public services of the US, the UK and Australia. For a long time most of us had probably given scant regard to this, confident in our assumptions about the political independence of our public employees. Now we understand much more clearly that our confidence was ill-founded, that in fact we confront a serious systemic problem. In essence, our political leaders have lost sight of the honest-broker role of their senior public servants and have become too keen to manipulate and pressure them into policy compliance. And our senior officials have taken the bait, now more than ever prepared to run with their government's political agenda.

The focus since the start of the Iraq war on the politicisation of the intelligence services in particular has been understandable, if somewhat misplaced. At every opportunity the architects of the war have sought to offload responsibility for the flawed official case for war onto the intelligence services. It must be remembered, though, that the spooks neither wanted a war nor made the decision to wage it. Governments make decisions based on many considerations and sources of advice; the intelligence agencies are only one small element in this process. Party-political ideological positions as well as personal beliefs and biases are important factors, along with the influence of key members of personal staffs, policy departments, polling, focus groups and media reporting. Even pillow talk is relevant, at least in the case of John Howard, whose wife, Janette, is acknowledged by the Prime Minister himself to hold considerable sway over his decision-making.

The influence of policy departments has received much less attention than it should have. What advice did the Department of Foreign Affairs and Trade give the key decision-makers in Canberra? By and large we don't know, and we will need to wait decades before the relevant documents are made public. If the picture is at all similar to what I saw concerning Australian border security, we should be worried. Take, for example, the heated debate among Australian departments in late 2002 and early 2003 over the Defence Force's desperate need to roll back its commitment to what it judged were unsustainable surveillance and interception operations. The Immigration Department chiefs resisted the move strongly (and unsuccessfully as it happened), not because the Defence Force's proposal was unreasonable, but because they were worried it would annoy the Prime Minister and the Immigration Minister, who were hell-bent on playing up their national security credentials.

Another example from around the same time concerns the debate within the inter-departmental people-smuggling task force about the increasingly apparent need to shut down the Australian-funded off-shore processing centres for asylum seekers – the one on Manus Island was virtually empty and a festering sore in the Australia–Papua New Guinea bilateral relationship, and State House in Nauru had degenerated into a lawless fiasco. In both cases there was no sensible reason to maintain the expensive and controversial facilities other than to market the government's national security credentials – a curious thing considering that no terrorist or suspected terrorist had ever been detected trying to enter Australia through that channel. In both cases the senior bureaucrats commiserated among themselves about the inevitability of the government's position and agreed finally not to confront it.

Such examples may seem trivial in comparison with the more dramatic politicisation of the public service evidenced during the Iraq war, but they are just as telling. It is heartening that at least some people in public service still tell it straight. How else to explain the dramatic last-minute dropping of charges in 2004 against the UK's Government Communication Headquarters translator Katharine Gun, other than as a result of the British government's concern that the presumably scrupulous advice provided by British Attorney-General Lord Goldsmith about the legal status of the war would have almost certainly been called for as part of the defence case? This would have been a bombshell, yet another nail in Tony Blair's coffin, because Goldsmith's advice almost certainly included a judgement about a war being lawful only if the threat posed by Saddam was imminent. This legal quandary probably also helps to explain Downing Street's fascination with the baseless claim that Iraqi

WMD were deployable within 45 minutes of an order to use them.

The politicisation of the intelligence agencies has two dimensions. First, politicians and their staffs put pressure on the agencies to deliver desired lines of reporting. Second, the agencies themselves develop a tendency to comply with the signals coming from government rather than resist them.

Occasionally the pressure on the agencies is direct and unambiguous, most often in the US. The US Vice-President, Dick Cheney, travelled out to the CIA headquarters on a number of occasions before the start of the Iraq war, in what my former CIA colleagues told me was an unprecedented practice. Imagine the scene – one of the most powerful people in the world sitting down at Langley with the spooks as they worked up their assessments on Iraq. Even before the Vice-President opened his mouth, the pressure on the CIA would have been overwhelming. There would have been no doubt about the purpose of the visit or the professional dangers that lurked for anyone courageous enough to challenge or disappoint him. In an atmosphere like that, it is unsurprising that key CIA outputs such as the October 2002 National Intelligence Estimate were skewed so badly – how badly is evidenced by a now unclassified excerpt which states, with 'high confidence', that:

Iraq is continuing, and in some areas expanding, its chemical, biological, nuclear and missile programs contrary to UN resolutions … Iraq possesses proscribed chemical and biological weapons and missiles … Iraq could make a nuclear weapon in months to a year once it acquires sufficient weapons-grade fissile material.[3]

Similarly there was the extraordinary personal involvement of Cheney's personal staff and then of Colin Powell himself in the development of his 5 February 2003 presentation to the UN. For four days Powell is reported to have worked through the detail of his speech with CIA officials before being satisfied it would send the right message to the Security Council on the eve of war. One version of these events was that all the painstaking effort was made in order to weed out questionable intelligence and produce as honest a case as possible. Now we understand, though, that just the opposite was the case, as evidenced by how much of the final version was blatantly at odds with the work of US intelligence agencies.

In the Security Council, Powell said that, 'Saddam Hussein is determined to get his hands on a nuclear bomb.'[4] Yet the Bureau of Intelligence and Research (INR), in effect Powell's personal intelligence assessment agency, believed quite the opposite. In the October 2002 National Intelligence Estimate it stated, 'the activities we have detected do not, however, add up to a compelling case that Iraq is currently pursuing what INR would consider to be an integrated and comprehensive approach to acquire nuclear weapons.'[5] In another example, Powell said, 'our conservative estimate is that Iraq today has a stockpile of between 100 and 500 tons of chemical weapon agent. That is enough to fill 16,000 battlefield rockets.'[6] But in September 2002, the US's Defense Intelligence Agency (DIA) assessed that, 'There is no reliable information on whether Iraq is producing and stockpiling chemical weapons.'[7] In essence, all the effort out at Langley in early 2003 was directed at producing a sales pitch, one to rival the equally extraordinary dossier released by the British some five months earlier.

In the UK and Australia the political interference with the

intelligence agencies was more subtle – not unexpected in Britain but perhaps more surprising in Australia given Howard's roughshod approach to dealing with the public service. Yet in each case it was no less effective. In London the Chairman of the JIC, John Scarlett, understood clearly what the government wanted and was quite prepared to deliver it. As already noted, the Hutton inquiry reveals that:

> Mr Alastair Campbell made it clear to Mr Scarlett on behalf of the Prime Minister that 10 Downing Street wanted the dossier to be worded to make as strong a case as possible in relation to the threat posed by Saddam Hussein's WMD ...
>
> I consider that the possibility cannot be completely ruled out that the desire of the Prime Minister to have a dossier which, whilst consistent with the available intelligence, was as strong as possible in relation to the threat posed by Saddam Hussein's WMD, may have subconsciously influenced Mr Scarlett and the other members of the JIC to make the wording of the dossier somewhat stronger than it would have been if it had been contained in a normal JIC assessment.[8]

At first glance nothing here seems particularly dramatic, but subtle things never do. The critical point is that, on balance, the JIC felt compelled to ignore the advice of its subordinate agencies in order to satisfy its political masters. The 45-minute claim remains the best unclassified example of this: the JIC signed off on a vitally important claim although it was based on a single uncorroborated report – in itself an unforgivable lapse in basic intelligence practice. Just as significantly, the JIC did so in a manner contrary to the urging of the most senior relevant expert in the Defence Intelligence Staff, Dr Brian Jones, who argued that the information not be expressed as a certainty but instead be carefully qualified.

In Australia the political pressure on ONA was equally subtle and equally effective. Everyone in the intelligence chain, from the Iraq WMD analyst through to the Director-General, understood clearly what the government expected of them, and they too were prepared to deliver it. The chain was a ludicrously short one: only a single full-time strategic analyst on Iraq, one middle-manager and the Director-General, Kim Jones. All three are decent people – two remain friendly to me – who most of the time adopted a commendably measured view on Iraq.

Except in one case: the marked shift made clear in the unexpectedly hardline ONA assessment produced in mid-September 2002 (later made public by the first Australian inquiry into the war in March 2004). This was an unclassified report put together at the request of the Department of Foreign Affairs. Specifically, the 13 September ONA assessment on Iraq stated that 'a range of intelligence and public information suggests that Iraq is highly likely to have chemical and biological weapons.'[9] It also commented that, 'there is no reason to believe that Saddam Hussein has abandoned his ambition to acquire nuclear weapons.'[10]

Yet only the previous day, the 2004 inquiry revealed, ONA had reported that there was 'no firm evidence of new CBW (chemical and biological weapon) production.'[11] Similarly, not much earlier it had observed that the evidence on the question of Saddam's nuclear capability was 'patchy and inconclusive'.[12] These findings had been contained in classified reports going to government in the normal way.

ONA's sudden shift to a more gung-ho position on Iraq is striking. For years it had treated the CIA's claims about Iraq with great caution and, along with Australia's military intelligence agency, the Defence Intelligence Organisation (DIO), it had continued to take a much more measured view than the US and the UK. What happened to change this stance? I believe the explanation is at its core rather simple. The Australian government's extraordinary request in mid-September for an unclassified report for use in the preparation of the Prime Minister's and Foreign Minister's speeches sent a clear signal to ONA to deliver something much stronger, something to back up the government's enthusiasm for war. ONA delivered, even though it propelled the Office into the fantasy land hitherto occupied chiefly by the CIA. Crucially, ONA is not a policy organisation and does not normally prepare unclassified notes for anyone's public speeches. The government's request for such a document in this case was a blatantly political exercise, regardless of how much or how little additional encouragement came with the request. ONA took the bait and responded with a blatantly political briefing note.

That the head of ONA was able to read the government so well is unsurprising. For years John Howard and Alexander Downer had cultivated the relationship between the government and Australia's top intelligence agency to the point where ONA had become as much a policy adviser as an intelligence source. The closeness has its origins in a coincidence. Kim Jones, the Director-General of ONA, had recruited Downer many years earlier, at the start of the Foreign Minister's unspectacular former career as a diplomat. But from this chance beginning there evolved a deliberate government practice of cultivating the relationship. The Director-General of ONA was even included in the Prime Minister's official party during at least one overseas trip. Such use of ONA, like the request for briefing notes in September 2002, clearly went well beyond its statutory role.

The cosy relationship made life easier for the government. I recall, for instance, being asked to develop an assessment on the situation in Afghanistan at a time when Australia was seeking to return asylum seekers there involuntarily. This I did. My report described a desperate situation – the new Afghan government controlled only Kabul; the provinces were still ruled by warlords and wracked by strife; returning refugees had overloaded completely all basic services; unemployment was skyrocketing; aid organisations were running out of money, and almost none of the international pledges of support had materialised. In essence, the fledgling nation was a disaster zone and was likely to stay that way for the foreseeable future. I reckoned this to be a useful report. Unfortunately, however, it was deemed to be too much at odds with the government's policy position on returning asylum seekers, and the assessment was shelved until it could go out in a watered-down version after the political heat had gone out of the matter.

Since my resignation, a number of other serving and former Australian officials have also voiced concerns about the performance of the intelligence services and the Howard government's relationship with them. Some of the most damaging assertions have come from Lieutenant Colonel Lance Collins, including the accusation that the Defence Intelligence Organisation only tells the government what it wants to hear. Collins is concerned with the politicisation of the intelligence services – the fact that the US, UK and Australian intelligence communities are reluctant to challenge their government's policy lines and, as in the case of Iraq, are even inclined to second-guess them and provide suitable findings.

Further, Collins' striking – and justified – accusation is that there exists a pro-Jakarta lobby in the Defence Intelligence

Organisation. Unlike Collins, I believe that the pro-Indonesia bias in the DIO is less a failure of that body than a long-term consequence of the Australian government's traditional reluctance to confront Jakarta. The DIO has gradually fallen into line with the pro-Indonesia sentiment of successive Australian governments to the extent that this sentiment has become a cultural characteristic of the key military intelligence assessment body.

Intelligence officers respond to this sort of environment in different ways. Most survive their early days in the job reasonably well, as the selection processes for employment in all agencies are sophisticated enough to ensure any squeamish applicants are weeded out at the start.

As in any workplace, however, the disillusioned eventually appear, bide their time, resign and move on. In the collection agencies, this may occur when they realise that much of their work is surprisingly mundane; in the assessment agencies when they learn that they have signed up to study every aspect of the dark side of humanity. For some, in any agency, the need to escape arises when they realise that their real work is concerned less with solving the world's ills and more with kowtowing to the will of their political masters, with all the dishonesty and opportunism that this can involve.

Others conform, play the game and get ahead, on course for the higher levels of intelligence agency management. Being rewarded for not rocking the boat has become so entrenched now for it to be regarded as normal. Public servants at all levels, including quite junior ones, understand clearly the importance of not causing problems, and those intelligence officers who stay for any period of time learn the secrets of survival and getting ahead. Operations are rarely bold; judgements are dumbed down; sharp edges are removed. Group-think is embraced to minimise the consequences of any error not avoided and, whatever the government's policy line, it is adhered to. The essential thing is to curry as much favour as possible.

I have several times been asked why I was the only serving intelligence officer in the US, the UK and Australia to resign in protest before the war. Sometimes the inference is that the uniqueness of my actions in some way discredits them. For some of my former colleagues, I suppose, the government's behaviour simply accords with their own political views. For the diehard Republican, Labour and Liberal supporters in the current US, UK and Australian public services, this is a straightforward matter. All are more likely to believe than to question anything said by the political leaders they revere. More subtly, though, the intelligence agencies have long tended to attract people committed to maintaining the status quo. Intelligence agencies still tend to be self-perpetuating, conservative creatures, and in practice this makes for a culture that is conformist in predictable ways. UK and Australian intelligence assessment agencies, for example, are strongly pro-US, so much so that they are sometimes incapable of providing scrupulous, disinterested advice about affairs in Washington.

In some cases there is inadvertent compliance with government deception simply because officials can't see through the spin. This is less incredible than it may seem: surprisingly few officials are aware of the overall picture when it comes to the broadest affairs of state. In regard to the intelligence assessments on Iraq, for instance, a country expert might work on the political situation in Baghdad, a WMD expert on technical matters, a military expert on the course of the war-fighting, a humanitarian expert on the possible consequences of war, and a strategic expert on the international backdrop. All this is as it probably should be, except that such a stovepiped approach inevitably leaves it to the senior agency staff – exactly the people most at risk of having become politicised – to draw the whole story together.

My intention is not to pillory my former colleagues. Most of them are good people. Some would probably have followed me out the door before the war, if only they felt they could have. But in reality most people find themselves constrained either by their sense of duty or by financial considerations – they cannot afford the instant loss of a career with little immediate prospect of another. Or else they feel powerless to make a difference and are overwhelmed with despair.

I was an exception on all three counts. My gathering concerns about the approaching invasion outweighed my sense of loyalty to ONA. I had the peace of mind of knowing that I could survive for a time on money my wife and I had accumulated over the years. Perhaps most importantly of all, I suspected that an individual in a place like Australia (or for that matter, in the US or the UK) could still make a difference – maybe not a big one, but enough to make the expected price worth paying.

Who is left to keep our democracies honest when the politicians turn feral and the bureaucrats roll over? The mass media surely has a role to play. Although it is in no way an official safeguard on political power in the US, the UK or Australia, it is nonetheless a powerful potential check on unbridled political authority. Yet this potential was largely unrealised before and during the Iraq war.

One of the worst offenders was the *New York Times*, which degenerated into a mouthpiece for White House disinformation, notably including the now-notorious 8 September 2002 article entitled 'US says Hussein intensifies quest for A–Bomb parts'. Rupert Murdoch's News Limited empire, in all its aspects, also distinguished itself as a vehicle for propaganda. The Fox News channel's fawning coverage of the US campaign in Iraq soon became a laughing stock. Murdoch's conservative broadsheet the *Australian* was no better. For example, on 10 July 2003 – months after the absence of any arsenal in Iraq had become evident – it ran the following headline: 'WMD doubts are ludicrous'.

In the end it was left to ordinary people to try to call their governments to account. In mid-February 2003 there was the extraordinary outpouring of public concern around the world. People took to the streets to express their opposition to a war in Iraq in numbers that almost defy comprehension. The authorities acknowledged that three-quarters of a million people marched in London alone on Sunday 16 February, while another hundred thousand or so protested in front of the United Nations in New York. These official numbers are certainly low – choose the organisers' figures instead and the totals can be doubled or more. Two million are said to have marched in London, at least a million in Rome, half a million across Germany, almost as many in New York and another third of a million across France. Some estimates put the total around the world at ten million. Whatever the number, the anti-war, anti-US foreign policy message at its heart resonated like a thunderclap.

Once I thought that anti-war activists were misguided. Even today, some hold views that are too extreme for my liking, and others are inclined to more mischief than I can approve. But I now think that almost all those who opposed – and still oppose – the Iraq war were just ordinary people with a strong sense of right and wrong. And I think, too, that in fact it was the pro-war mob that turned out to be misguided – some by their ignorance, racism, selfishness or apathy, others by their willingness to swallow whatever they were fed by politicians and a second-rate media.

The protesters helped to apply so much pressure that Bush, Blair and Howard were compelled to pursue the UN route much further than they might otherwise have done. This high-lighted the status of the United Nations as the world's pre-eminent multi-lateral forum. Moreover, the UN's eventual refusal to endorse the war in these circumstances effectively confirmed the illegality of the final US, UK and Australian position. That the UN did not buckle to the US's bullying and bribery, and endorse a war for reasons subsequently discredited, was probably one of the Security Council's finest hours. In the words of chief weapons inspector Hans Blix:

> The majority of the Security Council, which refused to authorize armed action, did not thereby make itself irrele-vant. On the contrary, it denied legitimacy to an action that should not have been legitimised: The grounds invoked did not exist ... how would we have looked upon the Security Council if it had simply said, 'Amen' to a request to author-ize armed action to eliminate weapons which did not exist? I think the authority of the Council is greater for not having allowed itself to rush to the wrong conclusions but urging longer time for inspection and examination of evidence.[13]

We do not know what Blair and Howard really thought about the unprecedented public opposition to their war. There should have been a palpable tension for them, caught as they were between a US President emboldened by majority public support in his own country, and widespread discontent in their homelands.

Perhaps they were not persuaded by the opinion polls show-ing the scale of the opposition, thinking that these would turn around once the war started (as some in fact did). Perhaps their focus groups told them that a steely, unwavering position on national security would be a greater political asset in the long run than any poll-induced change of direction. Perhaps – most likely – they realised at some point that they'd been lured into a terrible misadventure, but by then it was too late.

The millions of people who opposed the war were never going to stop it. George W. Bush was so determined to invade Iraq by late 2002 that no-one could have stopped it. But at least the protesters forced their governments into the position where they were exposed for what they really are – arrogant, unaccountable and imperious. This is a vital achievement, and a wake-up call to all of us that we must work even harder to mend our ailing democracies and punish at the polls those who betray our trust.

INTELLIGENCE FAILURES

*A great part of the information obtained in war is contradictory,
a still greater part is false, and by far the greatest part is
somewhat doubtful.*
—Clausewitz

The US, UK and Australian intelligence communities are not responsible for the Iraq fiasco. That dubious honour belongs to those who wanted the war and made the executive decision to wage it. George W. Bush, Tony Blair and John Howard – not their intelligence officers – are responsible for the illegal invasion of the sovereign state of Iraq without just cause. The blood of the thousands killed can never be washed from their hands.

That is not to say the intelligence agencies performed flawlessly. They did not, because to some degree they misread the threat posed by Iraq, and provided the stream of ambiguous and pliable information that was misused by their national governments when concocting the case for war. I don't claim to have done any better than my former colleagues in assessing the actual state of affairs. I too was sure that Iraq had a limited WMD programme; I am surprised that no weapons have so far been found. As it turns out, even my minimalist position, that Iraq had a disjointed and contained WMD capability which did not justify a war – for which I was branded naive after my resignation from ONA – appears in the end to have been an overestimation.

Iraq was a tough nut to crack for the thousands of intelligence officers assigned to work on it over the years. It was an authoritarian regime, and getting intelligence officers into places where they could observe things for themselves was virtually impossible. Recruiting trustworthy and worthwhile local sources was equally challenging: such people were rarely long-term informants, and conveying the material they had gathered out of the country was an uncertain undertaking.

No wonder, then, that the humint operations in Iraq developed a special character (comparable to the situation today in North Korea). The US, UK and Australian diplomatic posts in Baghdad were shut down long before the war, so these secure traditional bases for spy operations were unavailable. Occasional visits to the capital by diplomats did allow some insight into events, but such visits were generally far too infrequent, too restricted in their scope and too carefully supervised to enable any effective recruitment and running of local sources.

Denied their regular opportunities for spooks in diplomatic drag, the humint collectors were forced to look elsewhere. Allies who still maintained diplomatic missions were useful, although all sorts of baggage invariably accompanied their streams of intelligence and assessments. The French and German material on Iraq was always fairly good, but often not sufficiently dramatic – unhelpful, therefore, when it came to bolstering the official case for war being worked up in Washington, London and Canberra.

It was sometimes discarded, along with any other material deemed inconsistent with the big picture. Perhaps this helps to explain the divergent European approach to the need for war.

The Israeli intelligence on Iraq was much more useful. Tel Aviv had very good intelligence coverage of its arch-enemy, although the Israeli feed was invariably skewed heavily to encourage the US to think the worst. ONA was aware of the bias, as was presumably the Joint Intelligence Committee. Even so, such misleading reports were manna from heaven for those in the US, the UK and Australia who were cherry-picking the Iraq intelligence database for suitable findings.

Even more useful for the three countries was the intelligence provided by their agents and sources in the United Nations and other non-government organisations. Of these, UNSCOM and later UNMOVIC were the heavyweight spy outfits, riddled with dozens of intelligence officers and compliant officials. UNSCOM in particular provided Washington, London and Canberra with a vital means of understanding the situation in Iraq. There was nothing subtle about the misuse of the UN for intelligence purposes. That it was a shocking breach of the UN's independence did not rate a mention; it was apparently of no concern that stacking the UN with informants, year after year, was a blatant misuse of UN status. Nor did it seem to concern anyone that the practice gave considerable credibility to Baghdad's claim that the real business of the weapons inspectors was to spy on Iraq.

UNSCOM operated in Iraq until 1998, at which time it was abruptly and prematurely withdrawn by the charismatic Australian diplomat Richard Butler because of concerns about Iraqi non-co-operation. Before the pull-out, the weapons inspections were robust enough to allow for a confident intelligence assessment that almost all pre-1991 Gulf War Iraqi WMD had been used, destroyed or otherwise accounted for, and that any ongoing WMD programmes could only have been very limited if they had escaped detection.

The departure of UNSCOM and Butler from Iraq in a huff scuttled the intelligence agencies' best opportunity to learn about Iraq's alleged WMD programmes, and in particular about the status of any unaccounted-for WMD-related material. As I have already discussed, the suspected existence of such material should never have been inflated into a big issue given the relatively small quantities involved, the inevitable deterioration of any remaining Iraqi chemical and biological agents (except for mustard gas) and the significant uncertainty about the accuracy of the lists of unaccounted-for material. Years later, however, the proponents of the war took these same lists and rolled them into the central assertion that Iraq was in possession of a massive stockpile of WMD. On reflection, Butler's virtually unilateral decision in 1998 to pull UNSCOM out of Iraq was a crucial precursor for the war that would be waged five years later.

For the intelligence agencies at the time, the limited significance of the unaccounted-for material was reasonably well understood. It was regarded as an important intelligence gap, but not one in itself to warrant panic. Much more worrying was the absence of human intelligence after the departure of UNSCOM. Filling this hole was always going to be a challenge, not necessarily because Iraq was any tougher an intelligence target than, say, Iran or China, but because developing new intelligence-gathering operations in a hostile environment, especially for humint, throws up risks which need to be managed and counter-measures which must be overcome. Such operations require the devotion of substantial resources and take years to reach maturity.

Iraq was no exception to this rule, but something else arose to fill the gap: an ever-increasing flow of unreliable and un-substantiated intelligence from opponents of Saddam's regime desperate for US intervention and prepared to say almost any-thing to encourage it. Ahmed Chalabi and his Iraqi National Congress were particularly culpable in this regard, and the US was the major target. In the normal course of events, obviously biased, low-grade information is treated with great suspicion and often not even recorded on the intelligence database. Iraq was different: the imperative to come up with some intelligence – any intelligence – and the political pressure to support the case for war with helpful information combined in a rare way. In the lead-up to the war, this ensured that the established and proven intelligence vetting processes that normally serve us so well were applied much too loosely or even disregarded alto-gether.

The Pentagon's Office of Special Plans provides an extra-ordinary example of how the normal intelligence mechanisms and processes were butchered. This was a group barely known at the time in the US intelligence community and unknown in Australia. In theory it was a small band of free-thinking, hand-picked defence officials empowered to operate outside normal intelligence arrangements and given direct access to Donald Rumsfeld. In practice it became a renegade band of pro-war hawks. It was criticised by congresswoman Ellen Tauscher in the following way:

The concern is they were in the cherry-picking business – cherry-picking half-truths and rumours and only highlight-ing pieces of information that bolstered the administration's case for war.[1]

Dealing with poor quality human intelligence has always been a routine matter for the intelligence services. Many weird and wonderful reasons drive intelligence sources to co-operate with spies, including the cash routinely offered as an inducement. In Iraq between 1998 and early 2003 this problem of reliability became acute, as the proportion of dubious humint expanded rapidly at the same time as the threshold for its acceptance was driven down. Intelligence agencies were under pressure to back up the decision for war; political leaders were prepared to believe just about anything as long as it accorded with their pre-conceptions.

The available technical intelligence often also had significant limitations. Sigint is potentially a very effective form of raw intelligence, but it's useless unless the collection systems are cued properly. For example, sigint agencies prefer to have the phone number of a specific target in order to program the powerful computers that listen out for his or her calls. Nor does a phone number in itself guarantee success, because calls are not normally detected by eavesdropping satellites unless the relevant transmissions pass through an air gap.

Naturally, sigint agencies have developed processes and technologies to try to overcome such challenges. But Saddam's regime threw up many additional ones. Enough linguists had to be found to translate the enormous volume of sigint that was being collected. The Iraqis laid fibre-optic cables in an effort to reduce the output of signals able to be intercepted by the spy satellites. They used old-fashioned codes and couriers. In a secretive and paranoid country, there was an effective compartmentalisation of information that further constrained the liberal flow of sensitive communications.

These difficulties made Iraq a genuinely demanding mission.

The difficulty was further increased by the inherent ambiguity of much sigint. Take, for instance, the recording of a radio conversation used by Colin Powell during his 5 February 2003 presentation to the UN Security Council:

'Sir.'
'Yes.'
'There is a directive of the Guard Chief of Staff at the conference today.'
'Yes.'
'They are inspecting the ammunition you have.'
'Yes.'
'For the possibility there are forbidden ammo.'
'Yes?'
'For the possibility there is by chance, forbidden ammo.'
'Yes.'
'And we sent you a message to inspect the scrap areas and the abandoned areas.'
'Yes.'
'After you have carried out what is contained in the message ... destroy the message.'
'Yes.'
'Because I don't want anyone to see this message.'
'Okay. Okay.'[2]

According to Powell, this conversation took place on 30 January 2003 between a Republican Guard headquarters and an officer in the field. He said it was:

... all part of a system of hiding things and moving things out of the way and making sure they have left nothing

156

behind ... This effort to hide things from the inspectors is not one or two isolated events. Quite the contrary, this is part and parcel of a policy of evasion and deception that goes back 12 years, a policy set at the highest levels of the Iraqi regime.[3]

Perhaps this sounded plausible to many listeners. For some, nothing could beat the drama of such glimpses into the secret world of intelligence. Yet the recording, if genuine, was worthless unless accompanied by a string of detailed information, such as the source, context and reliability of the intercept. In the absence of such information, it was equally likely that the conversation involved nothing more than a well-intentioned effort by some Iraqis to check that they had complied fully with UN Security Council disarmament resolutions. Indeed, this innocent explanation now seems by far the most likely one, given that the intercept followed soon after the discovery of a small number of old, empty chemical warheads, and an Iraqi promise to double-check that no others had been missed.

Imint was equally incapable of filling the human intelligence gaps on Iraq. It's simply not that kind of resource, being little more than a way to take very impressive pictures from on high. As such, it reveals nothing about intention. In Iraq it could show whether factories had been rebuilt or the defensive layout of military units, but not what the reconstructed factories were actually producing, or what the battle readiness of the units was. Although it could fairly easily have picked up the sort of infrastructure associated with an advanced nuclear programme – had one existed in Iraq – this capability did not extend to tracking down the much smaller facilities likely to be involved in any limited chemical or biological programme.

Unfortunately, too, the imint collection agencies were some-times naive or simplistic, in a way that lent legitimacy to poor-quality or ambiguous intelligence. When a human source claimed that a particular factory was up to no good, some imint analysts felt that the identification of a good fence around the site and a boom gate was enough to verify the story. A tank for bulk liquids and a chimney for venting were counted as bonuses. Time and again this sloppy approach resulted in damning descriptions being attached to the wrong places. By the time Powell addressed the UN Security Council, even Iraq's fire trucks had been labelled as decontamination vehicles. And by the time the war started, it seemed that every second industrial, educational, medical and research facility in Iraq had been fingered as a suspicious WMD site. Not one of those places or trucks, or anything else for that matter, was subsequently found to have been directly involved in an active, offensive WMD programme. Bad humint created pos-sibilities that ambiguous sigint or loose interpretation of imint turned into probabilities.

That intelligence analysts can talk each other into absurd conclusions was made very clear to me during the WMD con-ference I attended in late 2001. We were trying to make sense of an impressive photograph of a concrete structure apparently close to completion at a foreign ammunition storage facility. It was an odd-looking building, with a distinctive roofing. Quickly the boffins decided that it was a high-strength testing chamber for chemical and biological weapons, and just as quickly most of the group nodded gravely and proceeded to discuss the implica-tions of the discovery.

Except that they were wrong. The mysterious structure was in fact similar to other conventional munitions bunkers in that par-ticular area – the distinctive roof was in itself of no consequence.

In other words, the high-tech photograph did not show that the building was associated with a foreign WMD programme. The idea that it was had never been backed up by any high-grade humint or sigint. There was nothing to suggest a WMD connection except the enthusiasm of the WMD experts that day to take their perceptions for the reality. Exactly this sort of reverse-engineering of potential threats occurred over and over again in relation to Iraq.

Everything comes back to the human element. This is where one finds both the real strengths and the undoubted vulnerabilities in the world of intelligence, and where some of the most important explanations are to be found for the overestimation of the Iraq threat. The report card on the human element is far from a perfect one. Ignorance, naivety and even xenophobia, together with knowledge of Saddam's track record and his continuing obfuscation, combined to skew the whole perspective on Iraq. Some spooks assumed the worst based on a broad range of unsubstantiated factors, none of which could be positively disproved in the absence of strong evidence to the contrary.

Unhelpful, too, was the common practice of recruiting generalist intelligence officers into many agencies, thereby often placing at the coalface young officers with little expertise in the frequently complex issues surrounding Iraq, and WMD in particular. Some young guns were understandably keen to take hold of any piece of dramatic news about Iraq and play up its significance. The initial excitement throughout the US, UK and Australian intelligence agencies concerning the discovery in 2001 of Iraqi attempts to purchase aluminium tubing from China is a case in point.

Effective intelligence exchange is one of the great advantages enjoyed by the 'Four Eyes' intelligence alliance (of the US, the

UK, Australia and Canada), turning its global intelligence coverage into much more than the sum of its parts. But on Iraq the exchange faltered, not badly so, but badly enough that questions need to be asked and problems remedied. The problem was probably most acute for Australia, given our almost complete reliance on the US and the UK for raw intelligence. Time and again the official statements coming out of Washington and London were apparently based upon raw intelligence unseen by anyone in Australian intelligence agencies. The problem was so serious that I felt moved to point out, in Laurie Oakes' original article in the *Bulletin*, that 'Australia has adopted a position ... based on incomplete information.'[4] So much for the Howard government's repeated assertion that sharing of intelligence is a vital reason for maintaining such a cosy relationship with the US.

The withholding of some US and UK information on Iraq from Australia was simply the result of error, but in other cases there was more than a hint of mischief. Swathes of the material obtained by the US and the UK would not have survived close scrutiny by a competent assessment body. Almost certainly this explains the extraordinary situation in the UK where the Joint Intelligence Committee refused to show to the Defence Intelligence Staff the single SIS humint report upon which the controversial 45-minute claim was based. So too, concerns for its own credibility probably explain the British government's refusal to share the mysterious intelligence it claims to have been given by another country which shows that Iraq did try to purchase uranium in Africa. The British explanation for not distributing this report holds no water: the claim that the SIS report was so sensitive that it could not be shared with another key UK intelligence agency is simply ridiculous. Just as bizarre is the idea that something so routinely flaunted as the 'Third Party Rule' was allowed to stop information as important as the Africa report being shared with the UK's closest intelligence allies.

In spite of the shortfalls in the 'Four Eyes' arrangement, there have probably been more successes than failures over the years. Few of course make the news or draw any credit, giving credence to the saying among spooks that there are only ever policy successes or intelligence failures. But Iraq in the end was a failure and one which, limited or not, should concern us. Too much is at stake these days to spend countless billions on capabilities which in the end may let us down.

No doubt the blame game over Iraq will eventually shed more light on the problems I have identified in the workings of the intelligence agencies. In the meantime we'll have to sweat it out and think through the implications for our future security, especially in the context of the 'War on Terror'. Some concern is warranted, given the inability of the intelligence agencies to foresee September 11, and their difficulty in tracking down Osama bin Laden.

Perhaps the biggest challenge facing many intelligence agencies is to come to grips with the rise of non-state, transnational security threats, such as the global extremist network linked to al Qaida. For agencies that grew up during the Cold War, whose operations are still geared in the main towards the targeting of nation states, these threats have proved to be something of an enigma.

During the Cold War the US and UK agencies had leads on Soviet citizens and ways of recruiting or otherwise getting at them. They were able to intercept vast quantities of the highest-grade sigint from the Soviet Union's communications network, and use their superior imagery satellites to monitor everything

from the vast complexes associated with Soviet WMD programmes through to more conventional areas of interest such as
airfields and military assembly areas. Decades were spent diligently tailoring a highly specific intelligence solution to the
challenges posed by the USSR, with the result that the country
was generally understood by Western intelligence agencies. I say
'generally' quite deliberately, because it is relevant to the limited
intelligence failure over Iraq to know that the real situation in
the Soviet Union after its collapse still came as a surprise to many
in the world of intelligence.

Terrorist groups are not countries. They are much smaller
targets for the lumbering spy outfits to find, track and understand. Fortunately, most terrorists are also bumbling fools, who
do much more damage to themselves than do the security services who hunt them. But not all are fools, and the success of
Osama bin Laden is testimony to the disproportionate effect that
can be generated by a bunch of fanatics with money and an
understanding of the operational security precautions needed to
sidestep the spooks. The al Qaida network is compartmentalised
both within and between groups, thereby reducing the risk of
loose talk and increasing the likelihood of controlling damage
caused by the compromise of operatives. Its members take care
when communicating by phone and email, preferring direct talk
when discussing sensitive matters and employing commercial
encryption and simple codes when using the airwaves. They also
think strategically, taking years to carefully assemble and train
operatives with clean slates, who are unlikely to be detected by
border security and intelligence officials as they travel about on
their business.

Since September 11, the US, UK and Australian governments have made much of their successes against al Qaida: a

number of terrorist plans have been thwarted, some operatives have been killed and captured, and a sizeable sum of funding has been identified and frozen. In the broader sense, however, these successes amount to little more than chipping away at the tip of an iceberg. Much uncertainty remains about al Qaida's long-term plans, while its dispersed international personnel and its financial and logistical base is essentially intact. Just as importantly, the extremist Islamic threat has now moved beyond al Qaida. Osama bin Laden's ideas have taken root globally, regardless of his future fortunes, and the numbers of those sympathetic to his views are swelling in response to concerns about US imperialism. The fall-out from the Iraq war adds powerful fuel to the fire. As I write this, I worry that we are currently losing the 'War on Terror' and will continue to go backwards as long as we remain distracted by Iraq, and as long as we continue to believe that terrorism can be defeated by overwhelming force.

When I worked on terrorism in 1999, a morning computer search for new material against a long string of key words including names and aliases of known and suspected terrorists might have thrown up only a handful of new reports, all of which could be scrutinised. By the time I resigned in early 2003, a similar search would produce many hundreds of reports, few of which could be reviewed in any detail in the limited time available. Even the biggest agencies, including the CIA, now struggle to deal with the flood of new information; much raw intelligence is now circulated virtually unchecked for credibility or merit. An increasing proportion of it was, and I understand still is, no better than what I would call garbage-grade. Yet such a stream of unsubstantiated titbits and gossip is easily cherry-picked by ambitious young intelligence officers wanting to make a name for themselves, or by their political masters, intent on playing up the national security issue for their own political purposes. The parallels with what happened in the lead-up to the 2003 Iraq war are truly frightening, making the need for review and improvement an urgent priority.

No-one wants, or can afford, to be caught out again as they were by September 11. As a result, worst-case analysis is increasingly taking priority over what is judged more or most likely. As with Iraq, the threshold for the acceptance of intelligence is being driven down at the same time as the proportion of dubious or unanalysed intelligence is growing rapidly. The US's enthusiasm for using force pre-emptively relies on good intelligence for any hope of success; but, as almost everyone now understands, this is not always going to be available.

Until relatively recently, the intelligence officers concerned with foreign intelligence were pre-occupied with traditional security threats. They shared their material with law enforcement agencies infrequently and only then in accordance with very strict handling limitations. This was done as much to protect the intelligence material as the crime suspects. It also reflected the historical, cultural and procedural distance separating the spies from the cops.

Fighting the civil offence of terrorism is now regarded by the intelligence agencies as its core business. Intelligence material is also used in connection with a raft of other transnational issues, including border protection, drug-smuggling, gun-running, resource theft and environmental degradation. Yet the new reliance on intelligence is accompanied by a widespread enthusiasm in government for throwing out many of the safeguards that previously protected their citizens from the practical and legal shortfalls in much intelligence material.

Such material, for instance, is not normally collected in accordance with the full range of law-enforcement procedures and requirements put in place to safeguard the rights of accused persons. Nor is it always collected in sufficient quantity to ensure high confidence in its accuracy. Moreover, intelligence sources, as we know, are routinely motivated by considerations that should probably preclude them from being regarded as wholly reliable sources of information. The threat of force to extract confessions is not uncommon in many countries; torture is still practised in some countries regarded as allies in the 'War on Terror', including by the US as the revelations from Iraq's Abu Ghraib prison showed.

Using shared intelligence to go after terror suspects presents special problems for recipient countries, especially second-rung intelligence partners like New Zealand who often have little or no insight into, and no control over, the priorities and practices of countries passing intelligence to them. Problems arise when the intelligence provided by other countries is unaccompanied by adequate notes on sources and reliability – especially important given the terrorist practice of passing disinformation during interrogation. Moreover, the sharing of selected information puts recipient countries at risk of being deliberately or accidentally misled. The bottom line is that the intelligence database on terrorism is by now so badly contaminated with faulty and weak information that the greatest care must be taken when using it. Of course, this is frequently at odds with domestic and international imperatives to be seen to be making progress in the 'War on Terror'.

I've been harsh in my assessment of the performance of the intelligence services over Iraq, and by implication this criticism extends to my former colleagues as well as to myself. I have done this deliberately and without apology, because I believe that organisations which fail to admit weakness win only pyrrhic victories, while those unprepared constantly to re-invent themselves are bound eventually to fail catastrophically.

SILENCING DISSENT

We must dare to think about 'unthinkable things' because when things become unthinkable, thinking stops and action becomes mindless.
—James W. Fulbright

Hearing in mid-2003 that Dr David Kelly was dead chilled me to the bone. One of the most distinguished experts on WMD in the world, Kelly had been caught in a no-man's-land between the British government and the BBC during their feud over the veracity of the official case for war. Now he was dead, found eventually in a lonely paddock not far from his home in Oxfordshire, another apparent victim of the Iraq war.

I'd never thought much about my own safety until that time, although over the preceding months a number of well-wishers had encouraged me to be careful in light of my attacks on the government. But on that mid-July morning I was a long way from home – in Washington as a guest of some former CIA colleagues – and on being woken by a phone call from a journalist in the UK advising me of Kelly's death, I suddenly felt very lonely, and a bit vulnerable.

Lord Hutton would later find that:

> Dr Kelly took his own life and that the principal cause of death was bleeding from incised wounds to his left wrist which Dr Kelly had inflicted on himself with the knife found beside his body ... no other person was involved in the death.[1]

Standing by the bedside that morning, though, matters weren't nearly so clear, and my head began to spin. Had Kelly committed suicide? Was he murdered? Should I be worried about my own safety, especially given my vocal presence in the US capital? I didn't know the answers, and in any case there were few precautions I could take. I assumed I didn't need to worry about an official roughing up, at least not by the Australian government, but kooks are a problem anywhere, and who could tell at the best of times what was really going on in some of the dark corners of the US and the UK administrations? Back home, I could be sure that a good number of Australians despised me. At times John Howard and Alexander Downer have probably wished me dead and gone, given the way my whistleblowing has threatened to spoil their lovely war. But fortunately for me, if not for the tens of thousands of Iraqi casualties, it is still much easier in democracies like Australia for leaders to kill en masse than it is to silence a single dissident.

The first official attempt to shut me up was weak – a statement delivered by the head of ONA within an hour or so of my resignation asserting, in essence, that I was a member of a branch unrelated to Iraq matters and normally only worked on illegal immigration issues. In other words, I knew next to nothing about Iraq, WMD, terrorism or much else for that matter. This was so far off the mark that it was easy to disprove, except maybe to those in the rusted-on, pro-war lobby.

For a start, I'd been a Senior Analyst – one of only a dozen or so at that level in ONA – with a Top Secret PV clearance. My access to intelligence included all the normal flow of material plus the additional Gamma and Echo category material, two of the most sensitive and closely held forms of intelligence. I'd been awarded a Superior rating in my last performance appraisal – only a handful (if that) in ONA had scored a higher rating. Not long before I resigned I'd been informed by the Deputy Director-General that thought was being given to my being promoted.

Because of my military background I was required to be familiar with war-related issues; hence I'd covered Kosovo and Afghanistan and was on standby to work in the National Intelligence Watch Office once the Iraq war began. I'd worked also on WMD, including the preparation of relevant Current Assessments on the issue, and I had represented ONA at a number of WMD-related forums.

Furthermore, I was also involved in covering global terrorism issues. In fact, my task on literally my first day back at ONA in late 2001 was to work with ASIO on a project to develop a list of innovative terrorist attack scenarios. My competence in global terrorism issues was reflected in my selection from time to time as the ONA briefing officer on the federal and federal–state anti-terrorism co-ordination committees – called back then the Standing Inter-Departmental Committee for Protection Against Violence (SIDCPAV) and the Standing Advisory Committee for Protection Against Violence (SACPAV).

And finally, as the Senior Transnational Issues Analyst at ONA, I was involved routinely in matters relating to Iraq. This provided me with almost unrestricted access to intelligence on that country. In particular, my December 2002 assessment on the possible humanitarian implications of a war required me to research in detail the threat posed by Saddam Hussein.

Having obtained no traction with this line of attack, the government opted to get down and dirty, the next day leaking to the media a story that I was unstable due to a breakdown in my marriage and therefore should not be listened to. This attempt to discredit me was cleverer than the previous night's effort, given that I was in fact living apart from my wife, Simone, at the time. But again it was an ill-considered strategy, the sort of thing that only an overconfident politician or official might have dreamed up. Quite simply, it was altogether improbable that an unstable person had for years held down the top security clearance in the country's senior intelligence agency.

The explanation given to me by John Howard's Chief of Staff, Arthur Sinodinos, during a 20-minute telephone conversation later that day, was that it was all the work of a zealous member of the staff and that Howard himself had no hand in it. I didn't buy it. Sinodinos's manner was all wrong – there was no sign of regret or apology, just an exaggerated attempt to head off the accusation that his boss was involved. And in any case, no-one on Howard's staff was sacked for the outrageous slur against me, and I had to insist that Sinodinos ensure the media were made aware of the fact that the story was unfounded. I have no doubt that Howard was in on the attempt to discredit me. It's well known to insiders that his office – and for that matter, his government's entire parliamentary machinery – is controlled too tightly by him personally and by his senior staff for something so reckless to take place independently. The whole incident speaks volumes about the type of man Howard is.

The damage was done, regardless of the circumstances or the apparent attempt by Howard's office to retract the story. It was some consolation, however, that the media pulled back from the matter almost instantly. They were simply too busy with the rapidly unfolding, broader Iraq drama to pursue this line of spin.

The Howard government's public dealings with Lance Collins provide a recent footnote to this incident. Despite the serious nature of Collins's accusations, the Prime Minister and others fell over each other to praise the new whistleblower and state a commitment to deal with his concerns. There was not the immediate resort to character assassination that there had been in my case. Yet the pattern was much the same in the end. While the government was saying all the right things in public, its henchmen were going to work behind the scenes — talk circulated that Collins was less impressive than the media portrayed him to be, and official reports were used selectively to discredit him. For me, there was a sense of déjà vu about all this.

After its initial attacks on me, the government laid off for a time, buoyed, I suppose, by the surprisingly speedy capture of Baghdad and with it the end of what we might now call the 'initial phase' of the Iraq war. For the time being, there was too much gloating and backslapping in Canberra and elsewhere to worry about an ex-intelligence officer with an axe to grind.

In May 2003, events complicated for Bush, Blair and Howard: the official case for war began to unravel. No WMD had been found. Nor had any evidence emerged that Saddam had co-operated with bin Laden. Around this time the *Sydney Morning Herald* asked me for an opinion piece on the situation in Iraq, including an assessment of the quality of the intelligence underpinning the case for war. The timing of the article was excellent, and it renewed the interest in my criticisms, so much so that the British Foreign Affairs Committee asked me to give evidence.

I travelled to London on the unquestioning assumption that here, finally, was a real inquiry into the war. How naive I was. My time in front of the Committee was limited to about an hour. I was not permitted to make the detailed opening statement I had prepared. The general line of questioning from almost all Committee members was influenced heavily by their incredulity at my audacity in questioning the British government's decision to join in the invasion of Iraq. It was a very tough session, and I performed poorly. A friend said to me afterwards that I appeared ill-prepared. Maybe so, but it was more the case that I was tired and unnerved by the grandiloquent manner of most of the Committee members. Nor was I to be their last victim, for it was these same people who later played a part in pushing Kelly to his death.

It was not only the majority of the Foreign Affairs Committee who wanted to do me over in London. The Australian government also saw risks in my renaissance and sought to use my appearance at the inquiry as a means to discredit me once and for all. They put in a carefully crafted submission, designed to flesh out the original allegation that I knew virtually nothing about Iraq. This time it had some effect, because the Chairman of the Committee was able to prepare a series of cunning questions which, answered 'yes' or 'no' – the only answers he allowed – managed to create the impression that I was not closely involved with the situation in Iraq. For instance, he would ask a question such as, 'Is it true that you spent two weeks absent from ONA shortly before your resignation while travelling overseas researching transnational issues?' To which I could only reply 'Yes', although that particular trip in no way diminished my general understanding of the Iraq situation, which had been built up over many months, or the specific preparation I was undertaking in preparation for my posting in the Iraq war National Intelligence Watch Office.

My disappointment with my performance in front of the British Foreign Affairs Committee was ameliorated a little by the small victories I did enjoy. One particularly odious British MP claimed, quite ridiculously, that I was the first person to claim the British government's September 2002 dossier was wrong, and he demanded to know what the evidence was for this claim. With some sense of satisfaction, I held up my copy of the dossier in front of him and responded stridently that not one claim in the dossier about Iraq's WMD programme had been found to be accurate. 'That's my evidence!' I exclaimed to his evident displeasure.

The Australian government was none too pleased, apparently, by my trip to London, especially as it had attracted considerable media attention back home. If I could use the media, though, so could my enemies. I returned home to discover that the journalist Andrew Bolt had written a scathing article in Melbourne's Murdoch-owned *Herald Sun*. The article discussed the Top Secret Codeword report I'd prepared in December 2002 on the possible humanitarian implications of the war. Bolt argued that I should not be listened to because my judgement was flawed, as evidenced by the inaccuracy of my predictions in the classified report. 'So let's sum up,' Bolt wrote:

> Wilkie, in his one written assessment of Iraq, and in his
> real area of expertise, issued warnings that turned out with

hindsight to be very alarmist ... The war happened, all right, yet there were no refugees, and huge casualties. There was no flooding, no toxic gases from burning oil wells and no humanitarian disaster of any kind. Saddam did not unleash germ warfare or incite 'mass panic'. Nor is there any starvation in Iraq ... Wilkie, honestly using his judgement, got all that wrong. Yet he wanted us to trust his judgement on something he was not expert in – Iraq's weapons of mass destruction. And to trust him above all his colleagues.[2]

That Bolt's article was misleading was of little consequence to me. I knew that my assessment had done a satisfactory job of warning the government of some of the things that might have gone wrong in Iraq. Some of these things had come to pass, while others, fortunately, had not. Moreover the assessment was technically sound – all the possibilities it described were based either on credible intelligence from multiple sources or on expert understanding of Saddam's and others' behavioural responses to crises. One of the issues I highlighted was the possibility of dams being blown up to cause a humanitarian disaster or to block an invasion from the south/south-east. Although some dam levels were low before the war, this was still a significant concern for the intelligence community, one supported by credible humint and imint evidence of specific dams having been prepared for demolition. It also accorded with our detailed knowledge of Iraqi peace-time water diversion works, army war-fighting doctrine and engineering capabilities. And, significantly, it was consistent with Saddam's approach to the possibility of failure: when facing defeat during Iraq's eight-year war with Iran, he had pledged to leave nothing of value for the invaders.

Compare this with the British claim that Iraq could employ WMD within 45 minutes. The case for the destruction of dams was so strong that it simply could not be ignored, but even so the prospect of their demolition was clearly qualified as a possibility rather than a certainty. It was a 'could', not a 'would'. In comparison, the 45-minute bombshell was based on a single, uncorroborated report, it ran contrary to the view of many in the intelligence services, and it was pitched publicly as an unambiguous fact.

Bolt's access to the highly sensitive report is troubling in several respects. The leak of the document and its subsequent possession and use by a journalist are serious criminal offences in Australia. What does it say about the state of Australian democracy that someone would risk sensitive national security material in an effort to silence a lone critic? Almost 12 months after the event, no-one has yet been charged, nor does there appear to be any government interest in pursuing the matter beyond some belated and feeble police inquiries.

I know the reason for this foot-dragging. I have learned that Alexander Downer's office requested and was provided with another copy of the secret assessment in the days immediately before Bolt's newspaper article appeared. This is unarguable – all outgoing ONA documents are logged and there in ONA's records is an entry showing that in June 2003 the Foreign Minister's office received another copy of my December 2002 Current Assessment on the possible humanitarian implications of a war in Iraq. This is extraordinarily telling. ONA material is not held for any period of time by recipients, other than by some colleagues in other intelligence agencies, none of whom had a reason to leak material to Bolt. Any leaked copy would almost certainly have to be obtained afresh by the source of the leak.

Downer's office was the only recipient of such a copy before Bolt's article was published.

Others may judge if Downer was personally involved in this criminal offence. His feelings about me are well documented – in August 2003, for instance, he described me as 'an increasingly hysterical malcontent'.[3] In parliament during September 2003, he refused to deny that, 'neither he nor any member of his staff provided Mr Bolt with a copy of, a summary of or a briefing on the contents of that report'.[4] Bolt apparently had reason to feel confident that he could get away with such a brazen act – 'when I go through the only secret report that Wilkie ever wrote about Iraq as an Office of National Assessments analyst' are his exact words in his article.[5] It appears he knew he had top cover.

One of the reasons why the leaking of national security material must always be treated with the utmost seriousness is that it risks compromising intelligence operatives and sources. These people truly can end up dead if their cover is blown, and such a thing can occur more easily than people who are unfamiliar with the world of intelligence may realise – names and operations are just the beginning; specific intelligence may provide an opportunity to backtrack to the source of the information. The sanitisation of intelligence material for public disclosure is something done with great care and always in close co-operation with the originating intelligence agency or agencies. None of these safeguards is applied when a Minister's office leaks a document to a journalist. Those who do such a thing are playing with fire. Either they don't realise this or, more likely, they don't care. In either case their actions are criminal and should be treated as such.

This attempt by the Howard government to discredit me bore a striking similarity to the Bush administration's clumsy effort to punish Joe Wilson, the former US diplomat who travelled to Niger in early 2002 to investigate the claim that Iraq had sought to purchase uranium. His finding at the time – that the story was clearly false – was communicated widely in the US government and passed through the normal intelligence-sharing arrangements to the UK and Australia. The matter was closed, or at least so it appeared until Wilson went public in July 2003 – via a *New York Times* opinion piece – to voice his concern about the US government's subsequent use of the Niger story in the official case for war. This was a body blow for the Bush administration and straightaway the gloves came off.

White House officials circulated stories to the media discrediting Wilson's reliability and suggesting that he had only been given the Niger mission because his wife was involved in WMD work at the CIA. These were all lies: Wilson had been a senior and well-regarded US diplomat, who was more familiar than most with both Iraq and Africa.

The White House's vengeance didn't stop there. In an act of extraordinary foolishness it leaked – to the syndicated US columnist Robert Novak – the secret information that Wilson's wife, Valerie Plame, was an undercover CIA officer. This was a bombshell. The leaking of a spy's identity is a very serious offence under US law; like the leaking of national security material in Australia, it is a crime warranting a substantial jail term. Even so, someone in the White House was so sure of their position, and so blasé about the implications for the CIA, that they were prepared to throw Plame to the wolves.

The issue wasn't so much that Plame's life was put in danger – a consideration nonetheless – but rather that the White House effectively compromised every operation and every source that she had been associated with during her career as a spy. In response, every competent intelligence agency around the world would have run Plame's and Wilson's names through their computers and, in some countries, pity anyone who had got too close to them. That the White House caused the death of someone, somewhere, by outing Plame is unlikely. But it is not inconceivable. It should also be noted that the information collected by Plame over her career as a spy is now much less valuable; now that its original owners know that it has been compromised, they will move quickly to control the consequences of that penetration. It was clearly of no concern either to the White House that they were burning a valuable intelligence resource – agents under non-official cover like Plame are few and far between and become worthless the moment that they are outed.

I hold out more hope that those who outed Plame will be brought to trial in the US than I do that Alexander Downer's office will be called to account in Australia. Once moved to action, the US justice system is still robust. In Australia, dark clouds hang over the Howard government in relation to the rule of law, given its track record of dishonesty and its bullying of the Australian Federal Police.

In his findings into David Kelly's death, Lord Hutton was careful to absolve the British government of any responsibility. 'There was no dishonourable or underhand or duplicitous strategy by the Government covertly to leak Dr Kelly's name to the media,'[6] he said. The bland judgement fails to communicate properly the complexity of Kelly's circumstances and the British government's clear, though indirect, responsibility for his death. Kelly was a good man trying ultimately to do the right thing, who found himself in circumstances he probably did not fully understand and certainly could not control. According to the Professor of Psychiatry from Oxford University who gave evidence at the Hutton inquiry:

... the major factor (contributing to Kelly's decision to commit suicide) was the severe loss of self-esteem, resulting from his feeling that people had lost trust in him and from his dismay at being exposed to the media.[7]

In discussing 'whether the Government failed to take proper steps to help and protect Dr Kelly in the difficult position in which he found himself', Hutton allowed himself to be scathing about some of those responsible obliquely for the tragedy:

... it must have been a great shock and very upsetting for him to have been told in a brief telephone call from his line manager, Dr Wells, on the evening of 9 July that the press office of his own department had confirmed his name to the press and must have given rise to a feeling that he had been badly let down by his employer.[8]

No-one can really know or understand fully the terrible anguish that drove David Kelly to take his own life. It would not be right for me to suggest how he felt because we, and the circumstances we decided to create for ourselves, were poles apart. Kelly was not a particularly self-confident man. As his situation deteriorated, he withdrew into himself, especially after he stood accused of lying. By contrast, I am more confident and better able to assert myself in the face of opposition. Kelly tried to placate his conscience by dealing with the media covertly, after the war had begun. I decided to step out boldly beforehand, guns blazing. Ultimately, I think, Kelly found that he had started something that he simply could neither control nor handle. I was better equipped, thanks to my different personality, for the crazy ride that both of us separately took.

That is not to say that I have always found it easy to cope with an enraged government. When the Prime Minister and his lackeys attack you personally in the press and the parliament, it gets the blood pumping and brings a new focus to your thinking. It's not for the faint-hearted or for those in any way unsure of their claims. The difficulty of dissent is surely enough to deter many potential rebels and to break most of those who dare to take a stand. Certainly I've felt on occasions that I couldn't handle for much longer the circumstances I'd created for myself. It can take a lot of discipline at times to hold it all together and keep up the straight face.

What has given me confidence is the knowledge that my past offers no opportunity to discredit me, a fact established, checked and re-checked through three Top Secret PV clearances – one in 1999 before being seconded from the army to ONA for the first time, another before returning to ONA in late 2001, and a final one during 2002 as part of my interest in ASIS.

I readily acknowledge that I was a larrikin in my youth, in particular during my five years as a cadet at Duntroon, where I set some kind of record by incurring around 250 punishments, 175 of them on consecutive days. You name it and I probably got in trouble for it back then – including roughing up the anti-uranium protesters' camp site outside Parliament House, souveniring flags for the cadets' bar, giving junior cadets a hard time, smothering an instructor in shaving cream, and getting caught with a woman in the barracks. Eventually, though, I was deemed officer material and graduated as an infantry officer with many of the values and skills that almost 20 years later would encourage me to resign from ONA and survive the difficulties that followed. In the end I was, to some degree at least, the government's own creation.

After resigning from ONA I received gestures of support from many people. There was not a flood of mail, but there was more than enough over the months to reassure me that I was far from alone in my concerns – and to my continuing regret there was more than I have had time to reply to. Some of the letters were revealing, such as the words of encouragement from a number of serving intelligence and military officers, including some in very senior positions. Others brought me to tears, such as a letter I received shortly after my resignation which more than a year later still cheers and inspires me, and which I feel compelled to reproduce here almost in full:

> Just wanted to thank you, Andrew, for your courageous effort to put a little more hope and sanity into our world. Your news was like turning a corner and seeing a beautiful rainbow. I am an 82-year-old Sister of Mercy. My mother lost two brothers in WWI and the lives of the three others were greatly affected. I lost a brother and a cousin and three other brothers affected in WWII. I thought after Hiroshima and Nagasaki there never would be another war … Gandhi and Martin Luther King have proved there is another way – peaceful work for justice. Jesus pointed out forgiveness and speaking out with love when authorities are wrong … There is a price, but the world will never forget what these three great peace lovers did. I hope and pray your price isn't too heavy. Many I know are extremely grateful to you. You've been a light in the darkness. You and yours will always be remembered in my prayers. God bless, comfort and guide you. Sorry about the writing. I've arthritis in my hand, but I did want you to know you mean a lot not only to Sr … but to many.

181

Other gestures of support have been more fleeting but equally powerful. There was the taxi-rank marshal at Sydney airport who said nothing more to me than, 'You are a good man. You know what I am talking about.' Or the fellow British Airways traveller who approached me in the lounge at Bangkok airport and said, 'At least there's still some hope,' referring to my appearance at the British Foreign Affairs Committee hearing. Or the Qantas flight attendants on a trip to Darwin who said that they thought I was doing a great job and slipped me a bottle of red wine as a gift. These and all of the other occasions on which friends and strangers have wished me well – most often simply saying 'thank you', an acknowledgement, I suppose, of their feelings of power-lessness as well as of their trust in me – have been powerfully reas-suring and inspiring. I will never be able to thank these people enough.

Not all of the responses have been encouraging, of course. On balance, however, there has been relatively little to cause me offence, and the abuse has been restricted almost entirely to the newspapers, where a handful of predictable journalists and letter writers have called me everything from a 'blow-hard', whatever that means, to a traitor. Nasty stuff, but consistent with the trend in the pro-war commentary towards vitriolic personal attacks upon those who opposed the war.

Attacks of this kind have been encouraged by the deliber-ate strategy of the Bush, Blair and Howard governments to 'play the man', so to speak, whenever possible rather than make an attempt to reply sensibly to critics. The White House auto-matically sought to vilify Joe Wilson rather than deal with his informed assessment that Iraq had not sought to purchase ura-nium in Africa. In the UK, David Kelly was persecuted by the Foreign Affairs Committee – 'I reckon you are chaff,' exclaimed one Committee member. 'You have been thrown up to divert our probing.'[9]

The Australian government's personal attacks on me have been impressive by any standard. Speaking with parliamentary privilege in September 2003, Liberal senator David Johnston in a single diatribe described me variously as 'a fourth-grade operative', 'reprehensible', 'flagrant', 'extravagant', 'outrageous', 'grandiose', 'contradictory', 'incongruous', 'inconsistent' and 'unreliable'. And, so that there was no risk of misunderstanding, he concluded: 'Where is this man coming from? He is very unstable. At the very best, he is unreliable; at worst, he is flaky and irrational.'[10]

This was not the only occasion on which Howard would unleash his attack senators to do the dirty work while remaining at arm's length from the resulting unpleasantness. When in August 2003 I appeared before the first Australian inquiry into the Iraq war, I was grilled by Nationals senator Sandy Macdonald, who seemed to have been briefed in detail on some of my classified work for ONA, in particular the assessment I had prepared on the possible humanitarian implications of the war. 'You are obviously quoting from the report,' I said at the time, initially not realising that Macdonald was not entitled to see the report and that anyone passing him a copy had committed a serious criminal offence.

In response, the government denied that Macdonald had received a copy, saying instead that the Senator's questions were based only on my public statements. This was an incredible proposition: it was because Macdonald's line of inquiry was so specific and nuanced that I had felt compelled to point out his obvious knowledge of the report itself. Nor did Macdonald deny the charge at the time of my accusation.

183

Convincing no-one with its initial lie, the government shifted to the ambiguous explanation that Macdonald had not been given a copy of the report but had been briefed on it by Alexander Downer's office. How interesting – Downer's office once again implicated in throwing sensitive national security material around for political purposes, in contravention of the *Crimes Act*. And how interesting too that the associated police inquiry seemed to go nowhere, exactly like the inquiry into the leak of the same classified document to Andrew Bolt. None of this seemed to concern the Prime Minister – 'I will not be telling the Australian Federal Police how to conduct an inquiry,' Howard told the media. 'They operate quite independently.'[11]

More recently there was the extraordinary spectacle of the Australian government's savage reaction when Australian Federal Police Commissioner Mick Keelty linked the 2004 Madrid train bombings with Spain's involvement in the Iraq war. What Australia's top policeman said immediately following the terrorist attacks was this:

> ... if this turns out to be Islamic extremists responsible for this bombing in Spain, it's more likely to be linked to the position that Spain and other allies took on issues such as Iraq.[12]

Fairly obvious and, in my view, accurate. In response, the government chose to attack Keelty personally. Downer – again – made what may be the Howard government's most outrageous accusation ever, namely that Keelty was 'expressing a view which reflects a lot of the propaganda we're getting from Al Qaida'.[13] Even General Peter Cosgrove, the government's top soldier, became involved in the obviously political debate. Predictably he sided with the government, telling the media, 'I see the same intelligence as he's [Keelty's] seen and I disagree with him on this occasion.'[14] It was a particularly unsavoury incident, and may yet prove to be a strategic mistake of considerable proportions for the government, because in one reckless incident Howard effectively discredited all of his earlier efforts to deny that he and his government pressure the public service.

EPILOGUE

So, why make the choice to act conscientiously (even if it costs)?
Because we can? Because that's what it means to be human?
Because in the end all that we have is worthless if we cannot
have a good opinion of ourselves?
—Simon Longstaff

Blowing the whistle on your government isn't for everyone. It can turn your life upside-down, especially if you were a senior intelligence officer. But it can also leave you remarkably at peace, especially if you're sure of your concerns and self-confident enough to ride the roller-coaster that inevitably ensues.

I was always confident in my intelligence assessment that an invasion of Iraq in early 2003 would be unjustified. The country did not pose a serious enough security threat to justify a war, too many things could go wrong, and it was plainly stupid to use force while other options remained. I stand by these judgements. And the ride wasn't too bad, although sometimes I felt I was holding on like grim death.

When I think about my resignation from ONA just days before the start of the war, I realise that analysing intelligence is easy but that deciding how to deal with serious government misconduct is much more difficult and much more important. It's a decision about what value we give to questions of right and wrong, good and evil, in our life, and the choices that follow from this. Perhaps this sounds a simple matter, but when the moment of decision arrives, the events can seem so overwhelming, the prospect of the reaction so daunting, the potential downside so unsettling, and the unknowns so many, that the only thing to do is keep your nerve, resist the temptation to question your judgement and take that first giant step into the abyss.

In countries like the US, the UK and Australia, no-one should be moved to blow the whistle on their government – not if what the government says and what it does share a basis in truth and decency, and if the relationship between the government and its employees is genuinely built on trust. Neither, however, was the case when it came to the Iraq war – George W. Bush, Tony Blair and John Howard waxed lyrical about the righteousness of their cause, but in the end they were exposed as little better than many of those they attacked.

Iraq could one day be a much better place for Saddam's passing. With its wonderful people and enormous potential wealth, it could eventually regain its position as one of the most prosperous and sophisticated countries in the Middle East. Yet the wounds will take a long time to heal. Like many people, I cried for Ali Ismail Abbas, the boy who lost his arms and both of his parents to a US missile in March 2003, but I've also cried for the thousands of other victims of the Iraq war.

If only the architects of the war, especially those who mourned UN Special Envoy Sergio de Mello, had cared just as much for every other casualty, perhaps there would have been fewer body bags and coffins. But they didn't. The bloodstained pages of history are filled with such people: men and women with no understanding of the real risks and costs of aggression, or care for the consequences. There's no chance of them or any of their loved ones lying in the chill desert night air pissing themselves with fear at the sound of approaching heavy armour, or being gutted alive by razor-sharp shrapnel, or losing a foot or worse from a mine or cluster bomblet, or having the flesh burned from their bones as they sit trapped in their blazing vehicle, or ending up bulldozed into another mass grave along with the rest of their squad, or even of surviving the war, only to die slowly from a cocktail of depleted uranium dust and countless untested inoculations.

There was no danger of any of this happening to Bush, Blair and Howard, because the people who make war today are rarely the ones who suffer from it. Politicians make wars, not soldiers. The key advocates for the invasion of Iraq risked no more personally than their political fortunes, while the soldiers they despatched risked everything. And let us remember that it was mostly Iraqis who died.

Decent people can't just move on and forget about the Iraq war, no matter how much the architects of the misadventure encourage us to do this. The implications of the conflict are simply too significant, too worrying. Many are self-evident, such as the way in which the war has actually encouraged terrorism. Others will take hindsight to understand properly, such as the degree to which the war has encouraged the proliferation of WMD among countries desperate to deter US aggression.

Nor can decent people forget the dark side of our democracies exposed by the war, or that our so-called leaders have now almost completely abandoned social interest in favour of self-interest. Nothing is spared their imperial schemes. We were told Iraq had failed to disarm in contravention of UN Security Council resolutions – wrong. We were told the war would be part of the 'War on Terror' – wrong. We were told the need to resort to force was urgent – wrong. We were told our troops would be greeted as liberators – wrong. All wrong.

That we're still resorting to war to solve our perceived problems and to pursue our strategic interests is not only unethical but also stupid. Certainly, resort to force is sometimes necessary. I don't think many people would condemn the use of force to stop the genocide in Kosovo, or to topple the Taliban and deny sanctuary to al Qaida in Afghanistan. Many people remain dismayed that the international community failed to stop the slaughter in Rwanda. But the Iraq war was neither justified nor lawful. It became unforgivable with the first innocent victim.

GLOSSARY

AFP – Australian Federal Police

ASIO – Australian Security Intelligence Organisation

ASIS – Australian Secret Intelligence Service

ASPI – Australian Strategic Policy Institute

CBR – chemical, biological, radiological

CBW – chemical and biological weapons

CIA – Central Intelligence Agency (US)

comint – communications intelligence

DCI – Director of the CIA (US)

DFAT – Department of Foreign Affairs and Trade (Aust)

DG – Director-General

DGIA – Defence Geographic and Imagery Intelligence
Agency (UK)

DIA – Defense Intelligence Agency (US)

DIGO – Defence Imagery and Geospatial Organisation (Aust)

DIO – Defence Intelligence Organisation (Aust)

DIS – Defence Intelligence Staff (UK)

DSD – Defence Signals Directorate (Aust)

elint – electronic intelligence

FCO – Foreign and Commonwealth Office (UK)

GCHQ – Government Communications Headquarters (UK)

humint – human intelligence

IAEA – International Atomic Energy Agency

imint – imagery intelligence

INR – Bureau of Intelligence and Research (US)

ISG – Iraq Survey Group

JIC – Joint Intelligence Committee (UK)

NATO – North Atlantic Treaty Organisation

NFIAP – National Foreign Intelligence Assessment Priority
 (Aust)

NGA – National Geospatial-Intelligence Agency (US)

NICR – National Intelligence Collection Requirement (Aust)

NIE – National Intelligence Estimate (US)

NIWO – National Intelligence Watch Office (Aust)

NSA – National Security Agency (US)

NSC – National Security Committee of Cabinet (Aust)

ONA – Office of National Assessments (Aust)

OPEC – Organisation of the Petroleum Exporting Countries

SACPAV – Standing Advisory Committee for Protection
 Against Violence (Aust)

SIDCPAV – Standing Inter-Departmental Committee for
 Protection Against Violence (Aust)

sigint – signals intelligence

SIS – Secret Intelligence Service (UK)

UNMOVIC – United Nations Monitoring, Verification and
 Inspection Commission

UNSCOM – United Nations Special Commission

UNSCR – United Nations Security Council Resolution

WMD – weapons of mass destruction

NOTES

TAKING A STAND

1. George W. Bush, Cincinnati Museum Center–Cincinnati Union Terminal, 7 October 2002.
2. ABC, *The 7.30 Report*, 11 March 2003.

LIFE ON THE INSIDE

1. http://www.asis.gov.au/employment.2.html#Intelligence.

THE WORLD OF INTELLIGENCE

1. http://www.intelligence.gov/2-counterint_f.shtml.

AN UNNECESSARY WAR

1. George Wright, 'Wolfowitz: Iraq War Was About Oil', *Guardian*, 4 June 2003.
2. George W. Bush, FBI Headquarters, Washington DC, 25 September 2001.
3. Paul Wolfowitz, interviewed by Sam Tannenhaus, *Vanity Fair*, 9 May 2003.
4. Paul O'Neill, interviewed by Lesley Stahl, CBS *News*, 11 January 2004.
5. Richard Clarke, *Against All Enemies: Inside America's War on Terror*, New York, Free Press, 2004.

THE BIG LIE

1. *Iraq's Weapons of Mass Destruction: The Assessment of the British Government*, September 2002.
2. *Ibid.*
3. George W. Bush, Cincinnati Museum Center–Cincinnati Union Terminal, 7 October 2002.
4. George W. Bush, State of the Union Speech, Washington DC, 28 January 2003.
5. John Howard, Ministerial Statement to Parliament House, Canberra, 4 February 2003.
6. Colin Powell, UN Security Council, New York, 5 February 2003.
7. Mohamed El Baradei, UN Security Council, New York, 9 January 2003.
8. Mohamed El Baradei, UN Security Council, New York, 7 March 2003.
9. US National Intelligence Estimate, 'Iraq's Continuing Programs for Weapons of Mass Destruction', October 2002.
10. *Ibid.*
11. *Iraq's Weapons of Mass Destruction: The Assessment of the British Government*, September 2002.
12. Michael R. Gordon and Judith Miller, 'US Says Hussein Intensifies Quest for A-Bomb Parts', *New York Times*, 8 September 2002.
13. George W. Bush, United Nations General Assembly, New York, 17 September 2002.
14. Alexander Downer, Statement to House of Representatives, Parliament House, Canberra, 17 September 2002.
15. Tony Blair, House of Commons, London, 24 September 2002.
16. Joseph C. Wilson, 'What I Didn't Find in Africa', *New York Times*, 6 July 2003.
17. *Ibid.*
18. Charter of the United Nations, Chapter 7, Article 51.
19. *The National Security Strategy of the United States of America*, September 2002.
20. Department of the Attorney-General, advice to the Australian government, March 2003.

BLAME GAME

1. Colin Powell, remarks after interview with NBC *Meet the Press*, Washington DC, 4 May 2003.
2. Donald Rumsfeld, interviewed by Tony Snow, Fox *News Sunday*, 4 May 2003.
3. Richard Myers, NBC *Today Show*, 26 May 2003.

4. James Conway, live videoconference media briefing from Iraq, 30 May 2003.
5. Donald Rumsfeld, ABC *This Week with George Stephanopoulos*, 30 March 2003.
6. Andrew Wilkie, 'A Lack of Intelligence', *Sydney Morning Herald*, 31 May–1 June 2003.
7. George W. Bush, interview with TVP Poland, 29 May 2003.
8. CIA–DIA joint report, *Iraqi Mobile Biological Warfare Agent Production Plants*, 28 May 2003.
9. Colin Powell, airborne news conference en route from Europe to the US, 2 April 2004.
10. Stephan Lewandowsky, letter to Andrew Wilkie, 23 March 2004.
11. David Kay, interviewed by Julian Borger, *Guardian*, 3 March 2004.
12. David Kay, House Permanent Select Committee on Intelligence, the House Committee on Appropriations, Sub-Committee on Defense, and the Senate Select Committee on Intelligence, 2 October 2003.
13. Mark Forbes and Barton Gellman, 'Iraq Had No Bomb Project: Expert', *Age*, 27 October 2003.
14. *Ibid.*
15. David Kay, Senate Armed Services Committee, Washington DC, 28 January 2004.
16. Andrew Wilkie, interviewed by Laurie Oakes, *Bulletin*, 18 March 2003.
17. David Kay, interviewed by Julian Borger, *Guardian*, 3 March 2004.
18. David Kay, Senate Armed Services Committee, Washington DC, 28 January 2004.
19. House of Commons Select Committee on Foreign Affairs Ninth Report, 3 July 2003.
20. *Ibid.*
21. *Report of the Inquiry into the Circumstances Surrounding the Death of Dr David Kelly CMG by Lord Hutton*, 28 January 2004.
22. Peter Varghese, Senate Standing Committee on Finance and Public Administration, 16 February 2004.
23. Parliamentary Joint Committee on ASIO, ASIS and DSD, *Report on Intelligence on Iraq's weapons of mass destruction*, December 2003.
24. *Ibid.*
25. Kim Beazley, House of Representatives, Canberra, 1 March 2004.
26. Tony Blair, BBC *News*, 3 February 2004.
27. Tony Blair, PM Statement Opening Iraq Debate, House of Commons, London, 18 March 2003.
28. Tony Blair, Select Committee on Liaison, 8 July 2003.
29. Colin Powell, interviewed by the *Washington Post* Editorial Board, 3 February 2004.

30. Charles Duelfer, Senate Armed Services Committee, 30 March 2004.
31. Intelligence and Security Committee, Iraqi Weapons of Mass Destruction – Intelligence and Assessments, Section 126, September 2003.
32. Ron Suskind, *The Price of Loyalty: George W. Bush, the White House and the Education of Paul O'Neill*, New York, Simon and Schuster, 2004.
33. Richard Clarke, *Against All Enemies: Inside America's War on Terror*, New York, Free Press, 2004.
34. Jack Straw, BBC *News*, 15 March 2004.
35. Alexander Downer, Channel Nine *Today*, 16 March 2004.
36. Mick Keelty, interviewed by Jana Wendt, Channel Nine *Sunday*, 14 March 2004.
37. John Stevens, interviewed by Rosie Cowan, *Guardian*, 17 March 2004.
38. George W. Bush, State of the Union Speech, Washington DC, 20 January 2004.
39. Tony Blair, PM Statement on Iraq, House of Commons, London, 25 February 2003.
40. John Howard, National Press Club, The Great Hall, Parliament House, Canberra, 13 March 2003.

PUBLIC DISSERVICE

1. Senate Inquiry Submission by ONA, undated.
2. Mark Latham, interviewed by Michael Brissenden, ABC *The 7.30 Report*, 31 March 2004.
3. US National Intelligence Estimate, October 2002.
4. Colin Powell, UN Security Council, New York, 5 February 2003.
5. US National Intelligence Estimate, October 2002.
6. Colin Powell, UN Security Council, New York, 5 February 2003.
7. Bruce Auster, Mark Mazzetti and Edward Pound, 'Truth and Consequences', *US News and World Report*, 9 June 2003.
8. *Report of the Inquiry into the Circumstances Surrounding the Death of Dr David Kelly CMG by Lord Hutton*, 28 January 2004.
9. Parliamentary Joint Committee on ASIO, ASIS and DSD, *Report on Intelligence on Iraq's weapons of mass destruction*, December 2003.
10. *Ibid.*
11. *Ibid.*
12. *Ibid.*
13. Hans Blix, *Disarming Iraq: the search for weapons of mass destruction*. London, Bloomsbury, 2004.

INTELLIGENCE FAILURES

1. Ellen Tauscher, *Salon*, 16 July 2003.
2. Colin Powell, UN Security Council, New York, 5 February 2003.
3. *Ibid.*
4. Laurie Oakes, 'The Insider', *Bulletin*, 12 March 2003.

SILENCING DISSENT

1. *Report of the Inquiry into the Circumstances Surrounding the Death of Dr David Kelly CMG by Lord Hutton*, 28 January 2004.
2. Andrew Bolt, 'Spook Misspoke', *Herald Sun*, 23 June 2003.
3. Alexander Downer, 'Govt Moves To Discredit Ex-Intelligence Officer', ABC News Online, 23 August 2003.
4. Kevin Rudd, House of Representatives, Canberra, 16 September 2003.
5. Andrew Bolt, 'Spook Misspoke', *Herald Sun*, 23 June 2003.
6. *Report of the Inquiry into the Circumstances Surrounding the Death of Dr David Kelly CMG by Lord Hutton*, 28 January 2004.
7. *Ibid.*
8. *Ibid.*
9. Dr Kelly before the British Foreign Affairs Committee, London, 15 July 2003.
10. David Johnston, Senate, Canberra, 10 September 2003.
11. John Howard, 10 September 2003.
12. Mick Keelty, Channel Nine *Sunday*, 14 March 2004.
13. Alexander Downer, *Lateline*, ABC online, 16 March 2004.
14. Peter Cosgrove, *Lateline*, ABC online, 16 March 2004.

INDEX